# CHURCH AND STATE

## IN THE

# UNITED STATES.

# CHURCH AND STATE

IN THE

# UNITED STATES;

WITH

AN APPENDIX ON THE GERMAN POPULATION.

BY

JOSEPH P. THOMPSON.

FRED B. ROTHMAN & CO.
*Littleton, Colorado*

1990

Library of Congress Cataloging-in-Publication Data

Thompson, Joseph Parrish, 1819-1879.
    Church and state in the United States : with an appendix on the
German population / by Joseph P. Thompson.
        p.    cm.
    Reprint. Originally published: Boston : J.R. Osgood, 1873.
    ISBN 0-8377-1216-5 (alk. paper) : $22.50
    1. Church and state--United States.   2. United States--Church
history.   3. Germans--United States.   I. Title.
BR516.T5   1990
322'.1'0973--dc20                                                90-32572
                                                                 CIP

 The paper used in this publication meets the minimum
requirements of American National Standard for Information
Sciences—Permanence of Paper for Printed Library Materials,
ANSI Z39.48-1984.

# CHURCH AND STATE

IN THE

# UNITED STATES;

WITH

AN APPENDIX ON THE GERMAN POPULATION.

BY

JOSEPH P. THOMPSON.

BOSTON:

JAMES R. OSGOOD AND COMPANY,

(LATE TICKNOR & FIELDS, AND FIELDS, OSGOOD, & CO.)

BERLIN:

LEONHARD SIMION.

1873.

Entered according to Act of Congress, in the year 1873,

By JAMES R. OSGOOD & CO.,

In the Office of the Librarian of Congress at Washington.

*Boston:*
*Stereotyped and Printed by Rand, Avery, & Co.*

AMERICANS who may read this book will have the goodness to bear in mind that it was originally addressed to foreigners, who have little knowledge, and perhaps less appreciation, of American ideas and institutions; and that it should be regarded as a rudimentary essay upon topics with which Americans may be presumed to be familiar. Every student of European life and opinions will readily comprehend how important it is to correct the misapprehensions, and to counteract the prejudices, which exist in even the best informed circles of Europe concerning American society,* and how patient and toilsome such a work must be. The coarse display of money, the crude boasting of material greatness, the swaggering assertion of an independence which is but another

* By the liberality of the Hon. Marshall O. Roberts of New York, one thousand copies of the German edition were placed at the disposal of the author for complimentary distribution to leading clergymen, to members of parliament, and to professors in the universities.

3

name for ignorance, have done much to excite in such circles a distaste for American character, and a disrelish for American ideas.

The best of America is too little known in Europe, — her development in science, art, and literature; her devotion to the Christian ideal in society and in the state; and her growth in that broad and noble culture which should best thrive in the generous soil of freedom. It is the quiet exhibition of such fruits of national life, the cogent array of facts which illustrate the product of principles and institutions in the higher civilization, that must rectify the opinion of Europe concerning America, and compel the respect of her statesmen and her scholars. If Europeans are apt to assume for their several nations a higher culture than will endure the test of honest and thorough criticism, Americans too often fail to appreciate the best constituents of their own worth as a nation, or to secure for these the estimate that they deserve.

The ideal of American culture should represent the catholicity of the Christian conjoined with the inflexibility of the Puritan, the cosmopolitanism of the man conjoined with the loyalty of the patriot, the courtesy and dignity of the gentleman conjoined with the fervor of the orator and the modesty of the scholar. For many years it was my felicity to have before me this ideal in the intimacy of a most sacred friendship; and, as I write, the name so deeply embedded in my heart rises spontaneously to my lips.   To

WILLIAM IVES BUDINGTON

I dedicate this attempt to vindicate the principles which he has embodied in his life, and to illustrate the sentiments which I have so often heard him express.

If this essay, to which I was compelled by the pressure of circumstances in Germany and by the impulses of Christian patriotism, shall help to commend the United States of the New World to the United Germany of the Old, and to further a good understanding between these two mightiest representatives of Reformed Christianity, I am sure there is no one whose encouragement will be more generous and ample than his, or more grateful and rewarding to

HIS LOVING AND ADMIRING FRIEND.

# PREFACE TO THE GERMAN EDITION.

IN publishing this little treatise, the author has no thought of discussing the relations of Church and State in Germany. A stranger should not meddle with the internal questions of a foreign country; and one who has enjoyed hospitality as a guest assuredly will not volunteer to advise his host how to regulate his household. But, in these days of international courtesies, each nation has something to contribute toward the general welfare of humanity; and the experience of the United States in the solution of great social problems may suggest principles and methods to other nations engaged in the solution of the same problems under somewhat different conditions.

This essay grew out of a conversation in a circle of learned, devout, and patriotic Germans, who requested that the information then communicated touching the relations of Church and State in the United States should be put in writing for publication in the German language. Afterwards the author was requested to compile the ecclesiastical laws and usages of the United States for the use of an officer of the Imperial Government, whose name is no less honored in America than in Germany.*

Copies of this manuscript were submitted to several gentlemen of official standing in Germany for comment and inquiry; and, to meet their queries, the whole was rewritten, with a view to a comprehensive and complete, though condensed, presentation of the subject.

For the neat, discriminating, and accurate translation of the essay into German, the author is indebted

---

* Prince Bismarck being absent at Varzin on furlough, etiquette forbade that he should sign official papers written during this interval; but he dictated the following note, sent under the seal of the Foreign Office, which was written by his Excellency Baron von Balan, formerly minister of Germany to Belgium, and now acting State Secretary for Foreign Affairs: —

BERLIN, Aug. 23, 1872.

REVEREND SIR, — You had the kindness to give Dr. Hepke, about a month ago, an exposition, written by yourself, on Church and State in the United States. The work was forwarded to Varzin; and Prince Bismarck now desires me to express to you his warmest thanks for the very valuable information which you have put at his disposal, and which he read with great interest.

I have the honor to be, sir,

Your obedient servant,

BALAN.

The Rev. Dr. JOS. P. THOMPSON, Berlin.

to the courtesy of his friend, Dr. Med. Curth.* The phase of the ecclesiastico-political problem through which Germany is passing is watched with intensest interest in the United States. Once more has the Reformation come to the front in a struggle with Rome, that must powerfully affect the future of Christianity in the entire world. Germany stands to-day, as she stood in the sixteenth century, the bulwark of freedom and of faith, the light of knowledge and of truth. May he whose name shall stand in history as the first sovereign of the new Germanic empire, and who to-day receives the congratulations of a grateful people upon his seventy-sixth birthday, live to see the unity which he has established perfected and secured against every enemy from within and from without!

THE AUTHOR.

BERLIN, March 22, 1873,
  (The Emperor Wilhelm's birthday.)

---

* The translation is so clear and so elegant, that the author recommends Americans who read German to consult it for a good style.

# CHURCH AND STATE

## UNITED STATES OF NORTH AMERICA.

———◆———

## SECTION I.

§ 1. *Provisions of the Constitution and the Laws of the United States concerning Religion.* — The Constitution of the United States of North America declares that " no religious test shall ever be required as a qualification to any office or public trust under the United States " (Art. VI. § 3) ; and also that " Congress shall make no law respecting an establishment of religion, or prohibiting the free exercise thereof " (Amend. I.).

§ 2. *Religious Liberty more than Toleration.* — These two articles embody all that is contained in the *National* Constitution upon the subject of religion ; but, brief as they are, they proclaim religious liberty, in the broadest sense, as a fun-

damental right of citizens of the United States.
This means much more than the toleration by law
of differences of religious belief and of different
modes of worship.   The civil government is not
to inquire into any man's belief as affecting his
qualifications for office, nor to concern itself either
for the support or the hinderance of any form of
religion.   Toleration denotes neither the freedom
of religion from State control, nor the equality
of all religions before the law : on the contrary,
it implies either a preference by the State for
some one form of faith or worship, though other
forms are allowed ; or the right of the State to
regulate the administration of ecclesiastical affairs
by the civil law.   In the etymological sense, toleration is the allowance of that which is not
wholly approved; and, in the ecclesiastical sense,
it means specifically the allowance of religious
opinions, and modes of worship, in a State when
contrary to or different from those of the established church or belief.   Toleration is a concession, in part, of that control over religion which
the State assumes to exercise, but which it so far
allows to fall into abeyance.   Religious liberty,
on the other hand, is absolute freedom of religious

opinion and worship, a vested right of conscience, not derived through any grant of the civil power.

The British Government affords a good example of the spirit of toleration. While it still upholds the Church of England as the Established Church of the nation, and a part of the "Constitution" of the kingdom, it tolerates all forms of dissent, and, of late years, has removed from Catholics, Dissenters, and Jews most of the disabilities which in former times adhered to subjects who were not within the pale of the Establishment. In Scotland, where the Established Church is Presbyterian, the clergy of the Church of England become, in turn, Dissenters. But in the United States there can be no Dissenters, for there is no Establishment; and no mere toleration of beliefs, since no one faith, sect, or religion, is preferred as a standard, but all religious faiths and forms are alike equal and valid before the law.

Liberty of opinion, liberty of worship, liberty in all matters pertaining to religion, is not a privilege created or conceded by the State, but is a right inherent in the personality of the individual conscience; and the State is pledged not to

interfere with that right. Such is the theory of
the National Constitution.

§ 3. *Laws of Particular States upon Religion.*
— The constitutions of some of the particular
*States* require a belief in the being of a God,
and in a future state of rewards and punishments, as a qualification for holding civil office,
and for testifying in a court of justice; but this
condition is fast falling into disuse. The States
of North Carolina and Maryland have lately
modified it; and other States, in revising their
constitutions, have abolished all religious tests.
The constitution of the State of New Jersey
declares that " there shall be no establishment
of one religious sect in preference to another;
no religious test shall be required as a qualification for any office or public trust; and no person shall be denied the enjoyment of any civil
right on account of his religious principles."
The tendency of other State constitutions, if
not their positive tone, is to the same effect.

In all the several States the establishment of
any form of religion is forbidden, either in
express terms of the constitution, or by positive
enactments, or by a sentiment and practice

which have the force of common law. Perfect religious liberty requires not only that every man shall be free to exercise his own faith (provided this does not disturb the peace nor injure the morals of society), but also that no one shall be taxed in any form to support the religion of another. An analysis of their constitutions, and of the codes which have grown out of them, shows that the following things are not lawful in any of the States of the American Union: —

" 1. Any law respecting an establishment of religion.

" 2. Compulsory support, by taxation or otherwise, of religious instruction.

" 3. Compulsory attendance upon religious worship.

" 4. Restraints upon the free exercise of religion according to the dictates of the conscience.

" 5. Restraints upon the expression of religious belief." (See Judge Cooley upon " Constitutional Limitations," p. 469.)

The Fourteenth Amendment to the Constitution of the United States, adopted since the

war of the Rebellion, may be fairly construed
to forbid any State to impose upon its citizens
a religious test for political office, so far forth
as the Congress of the United States can have
power over the legislation of particular States
in such a matter.    That article declares that
" no State shall make or enforce any law which
shall abridge the privileges or immunities of
citizens of the United States " (Amend. XIV.
§ 1) ; and further, that " when the right to vote
at any election, for the choice of electors for
President and Vice-President of the United
States, representatives in Congress, the executive and judicial officers of a State, or the
members of the legislature thereof, is denied
to any of the male inhabitants of such State
(being twenty-one years of age, and citizens of
the United States), or in any way abridged
except for participation in rebellion or other
crime, the basis of representation therein shall
be reduced in the proportion which the number
of such male citizens shall bear to the whole
number of male citizens twenty-one years of
age in said State " (Amend. XIV. § 2).

The right of the United States, under its

restricted powers, to interdict a particular State from disfranchising any portion of its citizens, might be questioned ; but the penalty of such a proscription is, that the State is made to disfranchise itself in the same ratio in which it disfranchises its citizens. The primary design of this amendment was to secure the fruits of emancipation, and to protect the freedmen from arbitrary legislation in any of the States. But the principle of the article is as sweeping as are the claims of citizenship. It is forbidden " to make or enforce *any* law which shall abridge the privileges or immunities of citizens of the United States." Now, the Constitution of the United States declares the absolute immunity of the citizen from religious tests for civil office, or places of public trust ; and, should any particular State impose such a test upon candidates for office within its bounds, it is highly probable that the Supreme Court of the United States would decide that such an abridgment of the privileges of the citizen was a violation of the spirit of the Fourteenth Amendment of the National Constitution, and therefore void. But no conflict upon this point

2

is ever likely to arise. It is more probable that the States which have hitherto retained a religious test for office will either abolish it, or suffer it to fall into desuetude. The unanimous sentiment of the people of the United States is that the State is not an ecclesiastical, nor a politico-ecclesiastical corporation, but, in its essence, is a political organism. " It belongs to American liberty to separate entirely from the political government the institution which has for its object the support and diffusion of religion." — *Lieber on Civil Liberty*, chap. x. p. 99.

§ 4. *Religion not a Shield for Vice or Treason.* — Though the theory of political society in the United States recognizes and guarantees liberty of conscience as one of the primordial rights of man, yet no one can be permitted to use his religion as a cover for vices and crimes against society, or for treason against the government. Such freedom of religion would place the community at the mercy of fanaticism or superstition ; would license Thuggism, and restore the Inquisition. Though no form of religious belief or worship, *simply as such*, can justly be proscribed in a free state, yet for reasons of public morality, or for the safety and order of the Commonwealth, the State may forbid and punish acts done in the name of religion ; as, for instance, polygamy as practised by the Mormons, the infanticide of the Chinese, or the self-immolation of Hindoo devotees. And upon the same grounds, though not as being in any sense the agent of the Church, or as having any religious function, the State may enact laws for the general welfare, which have also, in other relations, the sanction of religion. Thus, for example, the basis of the State is the family, — the true *norm* of society; and in Western civilization, as contrasted with the Oriental, society is based upon monogamy. Though marriage is treated by the laws of the United States as a civil contract, it is also regarded by the people at large as an institution of religion, and is commonly celebrated with religious rites ; each and every sect being authorized by the laws to constitute the marriage relation according to its own usages, from the simple declaration of the Quaker to the sacred ceremonial of the Catholic. But, whatever the mode, the civil law determines the conditions which give to marriage its validity, and designates the civil and ecclesiastical officers by whom marriage may be solemnized, and the formalities to be observed in order to its legal consummation. No church-officer can legally officiate at a marriage, unless he is authorized so to do by the law of the State; and, in thus officiating, the clergyman, equally with the civil magistrate, must conform in every particular to the requirements of the law. This service is not a prerogative of his office, nor a function of churchly authority; but the clergyman is, *quoad hoc,* an officer of the State. The record of marriages is usually kept at a State office. A valid marriage can be consummated without any religious service whatever. The State regulates divorce; and, from regard to the well-being of society, it permits only monogamy, and treats bigamy and adultery as crimes.

Now, the Mormons, on the one hand, have established polygamy as an article of their religion; and, on the other, the Free-Lovers claim the right of a mutable sexual alliance as a part of their personal liberty. But here the State steps in, and says, " Marriage has consequences that affect the welfare of the whole community. It implies parentage and offspring; and the State cannot permit relations between the sexes which may throw upon the community the care of children whose parents make no provision for the family and the home." And so, by that law of self-protection which inheres in society, as well as by that moral sense which justifies monogamy, the State can legislate against polygamy and fornication, though practised in the name of religion.

The moral functions of the State will be discussed in a subsequent section. These are alluded to here simply as qualifying the principle of religious liberty, or rather as guarding against its perversion. The State is not divorced from morality when separated from the Church; and the liberty of religion is not the license of immorality.

§ 5. *Judge Story on Religious Liberty.* — The grounds of the article cited from the Constitution of the United States, prohibiting an ecclesiastical establishment, are thus clearly stated

by the former Judge Story, one of the ablest
expounders of American law, who knew per-
sonally some of the framers of the Constitution :
" It was under a solemn consciousness of the
dangers from ecclesiastical ambition, the bigotry
of spiritual pride, and the intolerance of sects,
exemplified in our domestic as well as in foreign
annals, that it was deemed advisable to exclude
from the National Government all power to act
upon the subject. The situation, too, of the
different States, equally proclaimed the policy,
as well as the necessity, of such an exclusion.
In some of the States, Episcopalians constituted
the predominant sect ; in others, Presbyterians ;
in others, Congregationalists ; in others, Quakers ; and in others, again, there was a close
numerical rivalry among contending sects. It
was impossible that there should not arise perpetual strife and perpetual jealousy on the
subject of ecclesiastical ascendency, if the
National Government were left free to create
a religious establishment. The only security
was in extirpating the power. But this alone
would have been an imperfect security, if it
had not been followed up by a declaration of

the right of the free exercise of religion, and a prohibition of all religious tests. Thus the whole power over the subject of religion is left exclusively to the State governments, to be acted upon, according to their own sense of justice, under the State constitutions; and the Catholic and the Protestant, the Calvinist and the Arminian, the Jew and the Infidel, may sit down at the common table of the national councils, without any inquisition into their faith, or mode of worship." — *Story on the Constitution*, § 1879.

§ 6. *Mormons, Chinese, and Jesuits.* — In point of fact, a Roman Catholic has been Chief Justice of the United-States Supreme Court; a Jew has had a seat in the Senate; and a noted champion of the "Religion of Reason" against revealed Christianity has been a member of the House of Representatives. Since Judge Story wrote the above, the Mormons with their religious sanction of polygamy, and the Chinese with their heathen practices, have become quite numerous in the United States. Are these also eligible to office under the National Government? This depends primarily upon the fact

of citizenship. Formerly the distinction between the citizen and the elector was much
broader than can now be maintained since the
adoption of the Fourteenth Amendment of the
Constitution. Some States required that an
elector should possess a certain amount of property; others that he must sustain a good moral
character; others that he should be able to
read; and some made distinctions between citizens of different races and colors. The Supreme Court of the United States once decided
that citizenship means nothing more than
residence; and also that " a free negro of the
African race, whose ancestors were brought to
this country and sold as slaves, is not a citizen
within the meaning of the Constitution " (Dred
Scott *vs.* Sanford, 19 How, 393). But after
slavery had been abolished by the war, in order
to protect the former slaves against a curtail-
ment of their liberty by State legislation, and
to secure to them the right to vote, the Fourteenth and Fifteenth Amendments were added
to the Constitution, which aim to establish uniform and impartial suffrage.

As before said, it was questionable whether

the Congress of the United States had the right to enforce upon the several States a uniform law of suffrage. The American political system holds fast by two principles, — local self-government so far as this is possible, and a National Government of prescribed powers for the common welfare. Like the centripetal and centrifugal forces, or the foci of an ellipse, these two principles provide equally against centralization and disintegration. Having in view these principles, the new amendments declare that " all persons born or naturalized in the United States, and subject to the jurisdiction thereof, are citizens of the United States and of the State where they reside ; " and that " the right of citizens of the United States to vote shall not be denied or abridged by the *United* States on account of race, color, or previous condition of servitude."

These declarations are peremptory ; for they lie within the scope of the National Government. But, in addition to these, the Fourteenth Amendment, without coercing the States, presents a powerful motive to adopt impartial suffrage by subjecting any delinquent State to a loss of representation in the ratio of the citizens whom it shall deprive of suffrage. For example: Upon the basis of one representative for every hundred and twenty-five thousand inhabitants, the State of New York is entitled to thirty-three members of Congress. The State might restrict suffrage to persons worth half a million of dollars; but, supposing that there are only a hundred and twenty-five thousand such persons in the State, New York would then be reduced to one member of Congress, instead of thirty-three. This penalty of the Fourteenth Amendment applies equally to any condition or limitation which a State may impose upon suffrage, not only to a property qualification, but to any requirement of social standing, of religious belief, or of moral character, except where the latter is tainted with a sentence for crime. If a State should deprive Jews and Catholics of the right to vote, its own representation in Congress would be reduced in the ratio of the Jewish and Catholic male citizens twenty-one years of age to the whole number of male citizens twenty-one years of age in the State.

Of course, the Mormon by birth or by naturalization, and the Chinaman by naturalization,
can become citizens; and being citizens, then,
if the spirit of the Constitution is obeyed, they
could not be excluded from any office under
the United States upon the ground of their
*religion;* though, if their *practices* under their
religion were criminal or illegal, this would be
a disqualification under the general powers of
Congress to preserve its own purity and the
purity of the civil service. As yet, the Mormons simply occupy territory of the United
States. Utah has not been constituted a State,
and could not be admitted as such into the
Union without first purging itself of polygamy.

Every public officer must be bound by oath
to support the Constitution of the United
States (Art. VI., Sect. 3); and a foreigner, in
order to be naturalized as a citizen of the
United States, must take oath to support the
Constitution, and " to renounce and abjure forever all allegiance and fidelity to every foreign
prince, potentate, state, and sovereignty whatever," and particularly to that of which he was
formerly a subject. Under these provisions, a

Jesuit might be debarred from office if it were proved that he had sworn allegiance to the Pope as his superior sovereign; for the government of the United States cannot permit a double sovereignty upon its soil. The recusant Jesuit would be treated as an alien; but his exclusion would not be upon the ground of his religion. The Constitution of the United States permits no scrutiny of a man's religious opinions to the prejudice of his civil rights.

The ecclesiastical legislation of some of the States of the Union grew out of the relation of the Colonies to religion before the war of Independence in the last century, when the prevailing notions of the times still favored either a Church Establishment, as in Virginia; or the support and regulation of religion by the State, as in the *quasi* establishment of New York; or the administration of the State exclusively by members of the church, as in the theocratic system of the Colonies of Massachusetts Bay and New Haven. That previous colonial history, so important to the question of Church and State in America, will be considered in the following section.

§ 7. *Religious Liberty absolves from no Duties to the State.* — As early as 1635, Roger Williams, the founder of the Rhode-Island Colony, who has been called "the Father of Religious Liberty," made a vigorous protest against all meddling of the civil power with religion. It was feared by many that the absolute separation of Church and State, and the declaration of religious liberty, on the one hand, would cause the State to relapse into heathenism; and, on the other, would give occasion to Roman Catholics and to fanatics to set up their religious obligations against the authority of the State, even in matters of civil conduct. These objections were met by Williams with a pithy illustration, which covers all the principles of the case : —

"There goes many a ship to sea, with many hundred souls in one ship, whose weal and woe is common, and is a true picture of a commonwealth, or human combination or society. It hath fallen out, sometimes, that both Papists and Protestants, Jews and Turks, may be embarked in one ship : upon which supposal I affirm that all the liberty of conscience I ever pleaded for

turns upon these two hinges, — that none of the
Papists, Protestants, Jews, or Turks, be forced to
come to the ship's prayers or worship, nor compelled from their own particular prayers or
worship, if they practise any. I further add,
that, notwithstanding this liberty, the commander of the ship ought to command the ship's
course; yea, and also command that justice,
peace, and sobriety be kept and practised both
among the seamen and all the passengers. If
any of the seamen refuse to perform their service, or passengers to pay their freight; if any
refuse to help in person or purse towards the
common charges or defence; if any refuse to
obey the common laws and orders of the ship
concerning their common peace or preservation; if any shall mutiny, and rise up against
their commanders and officers; if any should
preach or write that there ought to be no commanders or officers, because all are equal in
Christ, therefore no masters nor officers, no laws
nor orders, no corrections nor punishments, —
in such cases the commander or commanders
may judge, resist, compel, and punish such trans-
gressors according to their deserts and merits."

The principle that the State should not meddle in matters of religion, or that the Church shall be free, gives the Church no pretext to set itself above the State or against the State in matters of civil administration. Religious liberty stands equally opposed to political bigotry and to social anarchy. A free Church in a free State does not mean an *imperium in imperio ;* much less the erection within a State, and under the charter of its liberties, of the vice-royalty of a foreign power to work against the State.

## SECTION II.

### THE RELATIONS OF CHURCH AND STATE
### BEFORE THE REVOLUTION.

§ 1. THE early colonial history of North
America presents problems in the religious and
social life of the people which perplex a foreigner. Hence even such studious and candid
authors as Dr. H. F. Uhden (" The New-
England Theocracy ") and Dr. J. Rüttimann
(" Kirche und Staat in Nordamerika ") have
fallen into some serious, though very natural
and pardonable, misapprehensions. Thus Dr.
Rüttimann (" Erster Abschnitt ") ascribes to
the *Puritan* spirit in New England measures
of severity against other confessions, which
were due rather to the spirit of the *age*, and
which were to be found equally in the *Episco-
palian* Colony of Virginia, though there proceeding from the opposite extreme of church
polity. He also overrates the power of the

clergy in what Dr. Uhden styles "the *New-England* theocracy;" though, in point of fact, this theocratic government was a peculiarity of the Colonies of Massachusetts Bay and of New Haven, and terminated in the latter as early as A.D. 1665, — twenty-six years after the founding of the Colony. Such misunderstandings are due to the fact that the North-American Colonies were planted with very different materials, and from widely different motives. Leaving out of view the Spanish and French settlements, the several English Colonies represented quite distinct phases of English society, character, and religion. In some, the spirit of commercial adventure and territorial aggrandizement predominated; in others, the spirit of religious faith and of missionary zeal. Some were the children of royal patronage; others, the offspring of religious persecution. Three examples of these different types of colonial organization will serve to illustrate the position of the State toward the Church previous to the war of American Independence.

§ 2. *The Church established in Virginia.* — The Colony of Virginia was the first permanent settlement of Englishmen in North America, dating from the planting of Jamestown in 1607. The charter of this Colony was vested in a " company of adventurers and planters," a commercial corporation which governed the emigrants with a royal authority through a supreme council in England and a subordinate colonial council of its own appointing. This charter enjoined the establishment of religion according to the doctrine and usages of the Church of England; and thus the two bulwarks of English loyalty — an aristocracy and a hierarchy — were set up on the soil of Virginia. Devotion to the Church was a test of devotion to the king, its " head and defender." With the growth of the Colony, parishes were formed, in each of which a minister of the Church of England was instituted by law, and endowed with a fixed salary, in tobacco, a glebe. house and land. (See " Autobiography of Thomas Jefferson," "Notes on Virginia " by the same, and the statutes cited in Hoffman's " Law of the Church.")

At the first, under the English Toleration Acts of that period, Dissenters were allowed

their worship under certain restrictions; but
in each parish all the inhabitants were taxed
alike for the support of the parochial church
of the established order. By degrees a spirit
of intolerance crept in, and religious bigotry
was inflamed by political animosities. During
the civil war in England, the Colony of Virginia,
which now had a legislature of its own, es-
poused the cause of the king against Cromwell
and the Parliament; and hence adhesion to the
Established Church was made a test of loyalty
to the Colonial Government, and nonconformity
was identified with republicanism and disloyalty.
The party in power had recourse to religious
persecution, which, as often happens, had more
to do with political policy than with questions
of faith.

In 1643, the Colonial Legislature decreed
that no minister should preach or teach, publicly
or privately, except in conformity to the constitutions of the Church of England. Puritans
were banished, and forbidden, under heavy
penalties, to re-enter the Colony. At a subsequent period, severe enactments were passed
against Quakers; and it was even made a penal

offence for any master of a vessel to bring a Quaker within the jurisdiction.

As late as 1705, acts were passed by the Virginia Assembly, decreeing that " if a person brought up in the Christian religion denies the being of a God or the Trinity, asserts that there are more gods than one, denies the Christian religion to be true, or the Scriptures to be of divine authority, he shall be punished, for the first offence, by incapacity to hold any office ; for the second, by disability to sue, to take any gift or legacy, and by three years' imprisonment without bail." These laws were by no means a dead letter. Many worthy Christians were thrust into prison for preaching without the authorization of the bishop; and, only two years before the war of American Independence, there were six Baptists imprisoned in one jail in Virginia for publishing their religious sentiments. Thomas Jefferson, author of the Declaration of Independence, and the third President of the United States, strongly urged the repeal of these acts of intolerance in his native State. In 1779, all forced contributions for the support of religion in Virginia were abolished, and the Church Establishment was thus set aside; but it was not until the winter of 1785-6 — ten years after the beginning of the Revolution — that an act for establishing religious freedom was adopted in Virginia, and the last vestige of State and Church was done away.

This act, with a long argumentative preamble upon religious liberty, is given in full in the Appendix to Jefferson's "Notes on Virginia" (Works, viii. 454); but the essence of it is in these words: "No man shall be compelled to frequent or support any religious worship, place, or ministry whatsoever, nor shall be enforced, restrained, molested, or burthened in his body or goods, nor shall otherwise suffer on account of his religious opinions or belief; but all men shall be free to profess, and by argument to maintain, their opinions in matters of religion, and the same shall in no wise diminish, enlarge, or affect their civil capacities."

After almost two centuries of Church Establishment, with the varying incidents of toleration and persecution, at last, through the influence of a civil revolution based upon the natural rights of man, Virginia was brought to

declare the inviolability of conscience in religion
as fundamental to liberty in the State. Religious freedom was no crude experiment of an
abstract theory, but a practical conception developed by long experience. In this view the
testimony of Virginia has the weight of history,
as well as the wisdom of philosophy.

§ 3. *The Church in New York.* — The early
colonial history of New York presents an example of State provision for the support of
churches without the rigors of an exclusive
establishment. New York was at first settled
by traders from Holland under the name of
New Amsterdam ; and the Reformed religion, as
set forth in the doctrine and discipline of the
Synod of Dort, was naturally maintained by
the emigrants, the colonial clergy being approved and commissioned by the Classis of
Amsterdam. In 1640, the West-India Company, which had the control of the settlement,
decreed that " no other religion shall be publicly
admitted in the New Netherlands, except the
Reformed as it is at present preached and practised by public authority in the United Netherlands; and for this purpose the company shall

provide good and suitable preachers, schoolmas-
ters, and comforters of the sick " (Documents of
Colonial History, " Holland," i. 123). This was
intended as a rule of order. But Stuyvesant, a
noted governor of the Colony, attempted to use
it as an instrument of oppression and persecution. He issued a proclamation (1656) forbidding preachers from holding conventicles not in
harmony with the established religion as set
forth by the Synod of Dort. He persecuted
Quakers with fine, imprisonment, and banish-
ment ; but the authorities at Amsterdam re-
buked the governor for an excess of religious
zeal, saying, " The consciences of men ought to
be free so long as they continue moderate and
peaceable. Such have been the maxims of
prudence and toleration by which the magistrates of Amsterdam have been governed ; and
the consequences have been, that the oppressed
and persecuted from every country have found
among us an asylum in distress. Follow in the
same steps, and you will be blessed." Every one
was to have freedom within his own dwelling,
to serve God in his own way ; and so the Reformed Church was saved from becoming an

agent of persecution in New Amsterdam, afterwards New York. The Colony even became an asylum of religious liberty.

§ 4. *New York under the English.* — When the city was taken by the English, in 1664, it was stipulated that the Hollanders should enjoy the liberty of their consciences in divine worship and church discipline ; and, though the Church of England was at once set up by the new government in every parish of the Colony, a public declaration was also made, that " no person shall be molested, fined, or imprisoned, for differing in judgment in matters of religion, who professes Christianity " (Historical Society's Collection, i. 332).

At a later period, however (1686), the attempt was made to put the Province of New York under the ecclesiastical jurisdiction of the Archbishop of Canterbury, and finally (1689) to treat it as belonging to the diocese of the Bishop of London ; and no minister was to be inducted into any parish of New York without the approval of said bishop. Parish-rates were also levied upon all inhabitants for the support of the Episcopal clergy. At first, these measures were accompanied with the concession of " liberty of conscience to all persons except Papists, so that they be content with a quiet enjoyment of the same." As the case then stood, the Church of England was the church recognized and sustained by the government. Other existing churches of " the Reformed religion " were allowed. Attendance upon the Episcopal Church was not made compulsory; but public dissent was not encouraged. In 1706, a petition " to exempt Protestants from any taxation for the support of ministers of churches to which they did not belong " was rejected by the government; and, at a later period, the claim of an exclusive legal establishment was set up on behalf of the Episcopal Church in New York, and, indeed, for all the Colonies. In 1759, the then Bishop of London, in a letter to the king, said, " The Church of England being established in America, the Independents and other Dissenters who went to settle in New England could only have a *toleration* " (Colonial Documents, vii. 360).

The claim of an original establishment was earnestly and successfully contested by Pres-

byterians and other Dissenters in the Colony of
New York; and the attempt to extend the
Episcopal jurisdiction of the Bishop of London
over the adjacent Colony of Connecticut, and
the apprehension of the purpose of the crown
to establish the Church of England throughout
the Colonies, was one of the causes that precipi-
tated the American Revolution. The evidence of
this has escaped the research of Dr. Rüttimann;
for he says, "Es beruht auf einem Missver-
ständnisse, wenn Laboulaye, in seiner Geschich-
te der Vereinigten Staaten (Bd. ii. 8), sagt,
'On n'avait pas d'évêques, et on n'en voulait pas
avoir.'" Here Laboulaye is quite right; and
the misapprehension lies with Dr. Rüttimann,
who mistakes the wishes of High-Church royal-
ists for the sentiments of the people. The
Assembly of the Province of Massachusetts, in
its instructions to its agent in London in 1768,
said, "The establishment of a Protestant Episcopate in America is very zealously contended
for" [i.e., by the arbitrary party in the British
Parliament]; "and it is very alarming to a people
whose fathers, from the hardships they suffered
under such an establishment, were obliged to

fly their native country into a wilderness in order peaceably to enjoy their privileges, civil and religious. We hope in God that such an establishment will never take place in America, and we desire you would strenuously oppose it" ("Life of Samuel Adams," i. 157). And John Adams, the intellectual leader of the Revolution, testifies that the scheme of creating an Episcopate over the Colonies "contributed as much as any other cause to arouse the attention not only of the inquiring mind, but of the common people, and urge them to close thinking on the constitutional authority of Parliament over the Colonies" (Works of John Adams, x. 185).

How the common people felt upon the subject may be inferred from a popular caricature published in Boston in 1769. It is entitled " An Attempt to land a Bishop in America." A ship has arrived at the dock with a lord-bishop in full canonicals, his state-carriage and appurtenances. He is met by a crowd, who carry a banner inscribed " Liberty and Freedom of Conscience," and cry, " No lords, spiritual or temporal, in New England." They are pelting him with " Sidney on Government,"

" Locke," " Calvin's Works," " Barclay's Apol-
ogy ; " and the unfortunate bishop seeks refuge
in the rigging, and orders the ship back to
England, exclaiming as he goes, "Lord, now
lettest thou thy servant depart in peace." Laboulaye said truly, " On n'avait pas d'évêques,
et on n'en voulait pas avoir." (See the original
in " The Political Register," 1769, and a copy in
Thornton's " Pulpit of the American Revolution.")

§ 5. *Religious Freedom proclaimed.* — That
this anti-prelatical spirit of New England prevailed also in the Colony of New York is evi-
dent from the fact, that in 1777, the year after
the Declaration of Independence, the new *State*
of New York in its constitution abrogated and
repealed all statutes and acts of the Colony
which " might be construed to establish or
maintain any particular denomination of Christians or their ministers ; " and also ordained that
" the free exercise and enjoyment of religious
profession and worship, without discrimination
or preference, shall forever hereafter be allowed
within this State to all mankind." Thus New
York, taught by her own experiences and neces-

sities, preceded Virginia in arriving at the same goal. From this broad declaration of religious liberty that State has never in the least departed.

In this colonial history it now remains only to consider the theocratic system so far as this was practised in New England.

# SECTION III.

THEOCRATIC GOVERNMENT IN NEW ENGLAND.

§ 1. It is well-nigh impossible for the German of the nineteenth century to comprehend the English Puritan of the sixteenth. One loves to associate with Luther a genial humor, a generous beer-mug, a broad and hearty humanity, a love of nature, a fondness for children and for social life, a cheerful temperament, — breaking forth in song, often rising to hilarity, — and a Christianity that was emancipated not only from the traditions of the Church, but also from the older traditions of the Rabbis, and from the law of Moses. In a word, with all his vehemence as a reformer, his boldness as a disputant, his heroism as a champion of the truth, his loftiness as a counsellor of princes and a leader of his age, Luther stands forth as the familiar man of the people, the personification

of the national Gemüthlichkeit. But the popular idea of the Puritan — often met with in
England and the United States, as well as in
Germany — is of a stern dogmatist, who would
compress human life, faith, and salvation, within
an iron mould of Calvinism ; a fierce iconoclast,
confounding art with superstition, and waging
war upon imagination as idolatry ; a rigid
censor of manners as well as of morals, pre-
scribing laws for eating and drinking, for dress
and behavior, forbidding the drama, the conviv-
ial game, the Christmas merriment ; a morose
ascetic, denying pleasure as a sin ; a sour-faced,
strait-laced, sanctimonious legalist, imposing the
code of Moses upon the consciences of Christians, framing severe sabbath laws, and, according to the caricature,

> " Hanging his cat of a Monday
> For killing a mouse of a Sunday."

This popular notion of the Puritan is largely
due to the court literature of the age of Charles
II., when the restoration of the Stuarts
brought in a flood of licentiousness to sweep
away the Puritan simplicity of the Common-

wealth. But when one considers what corruptions in Church and State, in doctrine and practice, called the Puritan into being, one can pardon to him a little of sternness in his theory, a little of asceticism in his life; and, when one considers what persecutions the Puritan was called to endure, he will see that an iron resolution against the excesses of churchly power was a need of the times. But a movement that produced a Cromwell and a Milton had in it elements of moral grandeur; and the strength and heroism of American freedom in Church and State are largely due to that stern faith and that rigid morality which the effeminacy of modern liberty affects to despise. " Civilized New England is the child of English Puritanism. The spirit of Puritanism was no creation of the sixteenth century. It is as old as the truth and manliness of England." — *Palfrey's History of New England*, vol. i. p. 101.

§ 2. *The Pilgrim Colony at Plymouth.* — Dr. Rüttimann, in his " Kirche und Staat in Nord-Amerika " (erster Abschnitt), attributes to all New England a form of theocratic government. This, however, was a peculiarity of the Colony of Massachusetts Bay, and of the Colony of New Haven until this was united with the Colony of Connecticut. In the Colonies of Connecticut, Rhode Island, and Plymouth, no such theocracy existed. This last — the oldest settlement in New England — was in advance of all other American Colonies in the principle that the Church should be entirely independent of the dictation of the civil power, and also in maintaining the purity of the Church itself as a spiritual body. Upon both these points, the Plymouth colonists, known as the " Pilgrim Fathers," were far beyond the great body of English Puritans.

Long before Luther's Reformation in Germany, there was in England an earnest movement for the reform of clerical abuses : the claim of the pope to present to benefices in England was resisted by Edward III. and his Parliament ; and, when the pope threatened ecclesiastical censures, the Parliament rejoined (A.D. 1390), that any messenger bringing such excommunication into the realm " should incur pain of life and members." In short, as Froude expresses it, " a rehearsal of the English Refor-

mation was witnessed at the close of the fourteenth century " (see 38 Ed. III., stat. 2 ; and
Froude's " History of England," chap. vi.). The
religious spirit of Wickliffe and of his fol-
lowers, known as " Lollards," leavened the
English nation. Nevertheless, the Church of
England was finally divorced from its allegiance
to Rome, not upon grounds of doctrinal belief
or of ecclesiastical practice, but by the personal
will of Henry VIII., who constituted the sovereign the head of the Church as an institution of
the State. The Church was not delivered from
corruptions in doctrine and practice by this
transfer of allegiance from the pope to the
king ; but the spirit of reform inspired by
Wickliffe was still working within the Church
itself. " The secession from Rome was sancti-
fied and secured by an honest, religious sense
widely diffused among the people ; " and by
degrees there arose a party known as " Puritans," who were intent upon purging the
Church of every remnant of Popish doctrine,
and every symbol of Popish worship. The
Puritans, however, as a body, had no thought
of separating the Church from the State. They

were reformers within the Establishment. Regarding the Church as a national institution, they looked to Parliament for the reformation of faith and manners; and when at length, in the contest of Parliament with Charles I., they came into power as a political party, they used the authority of law, with severe penalties, to enforce their own standard of morals and piety. They substituted " a domineering Presbyterianism for a domineering Episcopacy."

§ 3. *Nonconformists and Separatists.* — But meantime some of the old Puritan Reformers had advanced into broader and clearer light. When, in 1559, the arbitrary will of Queen Elizabeth insisted upon absolute uniformity of worship according to the rubric of the Established Church, some of the Puritan clergy openly refused to observe certain portions of the Liturgy, which they regarded as relics of Romanism (1563). For this they were styled *Nonconformists.* Many were silenced, or deprived of their livings; and some were imprisoned, or were banished under penalty of death. Most of these prescribed Nonconformists awaited in patience the coming of better days: a few, however, despairing of any true reform, or any real liberty within a church ordered and controlled by the State, withdrew entirely from the public churches, and met for worship in private houses (1567). These were now called *Separatists*, and were held guilty of schism.

§ 4. *A Primitive Church.* — By the study of the New Testament, these Separatists came to the discovery that the primitive Church was simply a company or society of believers in Christ; that it had no connection with the State, and no bishop or hierarchy, but was a brotherhood in which all were equals; that it consisted of those who were spiritually renewed through faith in the Lord Jesus Christ, and who evinced that faith by godly lives; that every such society of believers had power to choose its own pastor or teacher and deacons, — the only officers known to the New Testament; and that such several independent, self-governing churches were united together, not by civil or national bonds, not by territorial limits nor external jurisdiction, but by voluntary communion in the same faith and the same works of love. Not a few of these Separatists were seized, imprisoned, whipped, tortured, and even put to death.

A company of these Christian believers met together in 1606, at Scrooby, near Bawtry, in Nottinghamshire, England, and there, in their own words, "joined themselves by a covenant of the Lord into a church estate, in the fellowship of the gospel, to walk in all his ways made known, or to be made known, to them, according to their best endeavors, whatsoever it should cost them, the Lord assisting them." Here are the principles of personal faith, of voluntary association, of progress in knowledge and truth, and of heroic self-sacrifice. All that these Christians asked of the State and its Church was the privilege of believing and worshipping in their own way. This was denied them. To escape persecution, they chose exile, and in 1607 took refuge in Holland (first at Amsterdam), then the sanctuary of religious freedom. In 1608 these emigrants settled in Leyden, where their pastor — Rev. John Robinson, a man of great wisdom, learning, and piety — lies buried at this day. But they continued to be Englishmen in feeling and in language: and,

when times so far improved in England that
they could obtain a patent of colonization, they
resolved to emigrate to America; and, sailing in
" The Mayflower," they landed at Plymouth
Dec. 21, 1620, — a day now celebrated as
" Forefathers' Day."

Before landing, this little band of exiles for
liberty of conscience assembled in the cabin of
" The Mayflower," and draughted a form of civil
government, which was the germ of the re-
publican institutions of the United States.

Their charter authorized them to settle in
the upper part of Virginia; but they were
about to land far to the north of this, — in an
unknown wilderness, beyond the jurisdiction of
any government. So they made a government
of their own. Standing around the table in the
ship's cabin, they organized themselves into a
commonwealth, and pledged themselves to
make just and equal laws for the general good,
and promised to obey the laws of the majority
and the officers whom they should elect. There
were forty-one men in all, representing very
different conditions of life. Every one of these
signed this compact; and they then elected one

of their number to be their governor. This is believed to be the first example of a written constitution based upon the equal rights of men as members of the State. These men recognized one another as equals before the law ; and, as the foundation of government, they laid down the broad principle, that laws should be framed for " the general good," and should be " just and equal " toward all alike.

§ 5. *Church-Laws at Plymouth.* — As the Plymouth colonists were all of one faith, and were, in fact, members of one church, they naturally made provision for the support of religion from the public treasury ; and, as the Colony extended, they ordered that churches should be built and maintained in every town at the public cost. At a later period, when the peace and safety of so small a commonwealth were threatened by innovations, they passed laws compelling attendance upon public worship, and forbidding churches diverse from those already set up and approved, unless the consent and approbation of the government should first be obtained. Theirs was not strictly an established church ; but the pretext

for such restrictions upon the very liberty
which they came to establish was the preservation of a homogeneous colony and of a pure
and independent church.  They required, also,
that a "freeman," or voter in the town-meet-
ings, should be of good personal character, and
"orthodox in the fundamentals of religion."
Such regulations show that these colonists were
not wholly emancipated from the notions and
customs of their times, nor quite equal to the
occasion of proclaiming religious liberty to all
men.   Nevertheless, the Plymouth colonists
made a great step forward, and were never
betrayed into gross intolerance.  Though even
this most notable colony — the mother of civil
and religious liberty — was still hampered by
the notion that the State should provide for the
maintenance of religion, and should punish
blasphemy, profaneness, sabbath-breaking, and
heresy, as crimes, yet it did not, like later Puritan Colonies of New England, go to the opposite extreme of restricting civil offices and
privileges to members of the church.

The original Pilgrims were more just and liberal than their immediate successors.   In the

second generation, the prosperity of the Colony tempted mere commercial adventurers to join it; and these brought with them elements of discord, disorder, vice, and irreligion, that seemed to call for severe measures of proscription. Yet harsh laws passed in an emergency of public danger were repealed as soon as the excitement had subsided; and Plymouth was, in the main, a model of a well-regulated Colony. Some errors and excesses must be pardoned to the spirit of the age; these have long since passed away: but the essential work of the Pilgrim Fathers in the pure conception of the Church as a spiritual body separate from the State, and the pure conception of the State as a free Commonwealth, is fruitful in blessings to this day.

§ 6. *A Theocracy in Massachusetts.* — A few years after the settlement of Plymouth, the Company of Massachusetts Bay was chartered, and began the settlement of Salem, Boston, and their vicinity. Though this company was commercial in its objects, the first settlers under its charter were mostly Puritans; and their church-organization followed substantially that

of the Plymouth colonists. But these Puritans
of Massachusetts were much more inclined
than their Pilgrim neighbors to use the civil
power in matters of religion.

The English hierarchy had been their op-
pressor; and, should the Church of England be
allowed a footing in the Colony, it would soon
overturn those civil and religious liberties
which the colonists had come so far to enjoy.
In order to secure good and true men for the
offices of government, and at the same time to
insure the preservation of the church order
first established by the colonists, it was decreed,
" that, for the time to come, no man shall be
admitted to the freedom of this body politic
but such as are members of some of the
churches within the limits of the same " (1631,
Mass. Colonial Record, i. 87).

In the Colony of New Haven (1639) the rule
was likewise adopted, " that church-members
only should be free burgesses," and that the
Scriptures should be the rule of government in
the Commonwealth as well as in the Church.
The first intent of these rules was, not to set up
a divine right in the Church to rule the Com-

monwealth, but to provide a government of ideal perfection. It was the old dream of Plato, — to create a perfect republic, which, at last, he confessed could not come into being "until kings are philosophers, or philosophers are kings." In the end, however, this theocratic system tended to produce bigotry in the State, and hypocrisy in the Church; and, with the progress of experience, it was discarded. As early as 1648, the churches of New England, through a synod, declared that " it is not in the power of magistrates to compel their subjects to become church - members; and as it is unlawful for church-officers to meddle with the sword of the magistrate, so it is unlawful for the magistrate to meddle with the work proper to church-officers."

In this theocratic government Dr. Rüttimann imputes far too much power to the clergy. He says, " Ueber die Aufnahme in die Kirche, also auch über das Aktivbürgerrecht, entschieden in lekter Instanz die Geistlichen, die nur denjenigen den Eintritt gestatteten, welche sich über ihre GEISTIGE WIEDERGEBURT durch Einsendung eines schriflichen, zur Vorlesung in der Kirche bestimmten Glaubens bekenntnisses ausgewiesen hatten." But it was the Church itself, the whole brotherhood of believers, which determined by vote whether the candidate should be admitted to its fellowship upon this evidence of his personal faith and character. The government in Church and State was a spiritual democracy. The influence of the pastor, in such a case, was only moral and advisory; and the pastor himself was elected to his office by the church over which he presided. New England was never governed by her clergy.

In judging of the Puritans of New England, and of the theocracy which they established in the Colonies of Massachusetts Bay and of New Haven, one must be careful not to ascribe to the spirit of the men, nor to the influence of their faith, laws and measures which were due to the spirit of the age and to the political necessities of the hour. It is common to ring the changes upon " Puritan persecution " and " Massachusetts intolerance ; " and even so cautious and candid a writer as Dr. Uhden ascribes to a peculiarity of the congregational

theocracy " those peremptory measures for the
expulsion of every opposite tendency which
threatened to disturb the unity of the Church
and the State governments, or but to cripple the
efficiency of the latter" (Uhden, "New-England
Theocracy," chap. ii.). But measures which
Dr. Uhden ascribes to a stringent church
theory, and which he elsewhere characterizes
as religious persecution, were prompted by a
political necessity; and, singularly enough, this
action of New-England Puritanism in the seventeenth century is reflected in the German
Liberalism of the nineteenth. It is seldom
wise for one nation to criticise the internal history of another; and " those who live in glass
houses should not throw stones." Yet the
experiences of one people may serve to inter-
pret the doings of another. What the Colony
of Massachusetts Bay did to protect itself from
emissaries of the Church of England, and to
rid itself of Papists, Anabaptists, and Quakers,
was grounded in precisely the same plea of the
necessities of government, and the maintenance
of public peace, order, and unity, which to-day
is urged by the liberal press for the expulsion

of the Jesuits from Germany. And if this
plea is valid for an empire of thirty-seven millions, with an army of twelve hundred thousand, surely something may be conceded to the
fears of a handful of colonists who knew too
well the dangers that threatened them from
pope and prelate without, and from faction and
fanaticism within. They, too, banished suspi-
cious characters and dangerous agitators. Said
one of the Massachusetts fathers, "For the
security of the flock, we pen up the wolf; but a
door is purposely left open where he may
depart at his pleasure."

But there was progress in liberty. By the
charter of Rhode Island, 1663, it was decreed
that "no person within the said Colony should
be in any wise molested, punished, disquieted,
or called in question, for any difference of opinion in matters of religion which did not actually
disturb the civil peace of said Colony; but that
all and every person and persons might from
time to time, and at all times thereafter, freely
and fully have and enjoy his and their own
judgments and consciences in matters of religious concernments."

Such, in general, were the relations of the
Colonies to religion, with the addition of the
humane and impartial policy of the Quakers in
Pennsylvania, and the liberal tendency of the
Catholics in Maryland. But the fires of the
Revolution, which welded the Colonies together,
consumed the dross of establishment, of patron-
age, and of theocracy, and left the pure gold
of religious liberty to be wrought into the
National Constitution.

## SECTION IV.

§ 1. *Relation of the Churches to the Laws.* — Since the Revolution which terminated the dependence of the American Colonies upon Great Britain, the theory of the civil government in the United States has been, that churches should be known to the laws, not as religious bodies constituted to maintain a creed and a worship, but simply as corporations empowered to hold property for religious uses. All rights of property which had been acquired by churches under the colonial governments were confirmed by the States which succeeded to their jurisdiction. The separation of the Church from the State, while it deprived the Church, for the future, of the benefit of State grants or taxes, did not work the confiscation of any possessions already held by the Church. For example, the first constitution of the State of New York, adopted in 1777, declared that "nothing

in the constitution contained should be construed to affect any grants of lands within the
State made by the authority of the king or his
predecessors, or to annul any charters to bodies
politic, by him or them, or any of them, made
prior to the 14th of October, 1775." This
covered church-property as well as educational
or charitable foundations and private possessions.

In the founding of the Colony of Virginia, as
has already been stated, the religious Establishment of England was adopted; and, before the
Revolution, the Episcopal Church had become
vested, by grants of the crown or colony, with
large properties, which continued in its possession after the constitution of the State had forbidden the creation or continuance of any
religious establishment possessed of exclusive
rights or privileges, or the compelling the citizens to worship under a stipulated form or discipline, or to pay taxes to those whose creed
they could not conscientiously believe. By
statute, in 1801, the legislature asserted their
right to all the property of the Episcopal Church
in the respective parishes of the State ; and

directed and authorized the overseers of the
poor and their successors in each parish,
wherein any glebe land was vacant or should
become so, to sell the same, and appropriate the
proceeds to the use of the poor of the parish.
By this act the State sought, in effect, *to resume
grants made by the sovereignty.* The Supreme
Court of the United States held the grant not
revocable, and that the legislative act was,
therefore, unconstitutional and void (Cooley
on " Constitutional Limitations," chap. ix.
p. 275).

§ 2. *How Church Property is held.* — But, in
order to hold property, each church must
either itself be constituted, or must cause to be
constituted as its representative, a *corporation*
known to the civil law. The mode of constituting such corporations differs in different
States; and also, in the same State, there may
be different ways of creating a church corporation adapted to different forms of ecclesiastical organization : but the principle is
universal, that the State does not know the
Church in matters of religious doctrines or
usages, but only in matters of temporal con-

cern. It has been ruled by the highest courts in the United States, that " the civil tribunals possess no authority whatever to determine on ecclesiastical matters, on questions of heresy, or what is orthodox in matters of belief; and so the ecclesiastical authority may not entertain any civil questions, or in any manner affect a disposition of property by the decisions of their judicatories. The court cannot interfere with the determination of the majority in any manner, except to correct a misappropriation of trust-property or funds " (Wilson *vs.* the Presbyterian Church of John's Island, S.C.).

In case of a dispute for the possession of church-property, the civil court might inquire into the religious beliefs and practices of the contestants, simply as *a question of fact*, to assist in determining the claim, precisely as it would do in the case of any club or voluntary association having a declaration of principles, or articles of agreement, upon the due observance of which the possession of a certain property was dependent; but only upon such collateral questions of civil rights does American law take cognizance of churches.

§ 3. *Test Cases under this Principle.* — Several
important cases arising in different States, and
under different forms of church polity, have
settled this as the uniform principle. In the
year 1810, in the city of Boston, and, to a wide
extent, in the State of Massachusetts, churches
that had been constituted upon a Calvinistic
creed went over to Unitarianism. Of the 361
Congregational churches then existing in that
State, 96 thus changed the basis of their faith.
In some instances, a majority of the Church
proper (that is, of those enrolled as communicants or members of the spiritual body) voted
to adopt this change of faith. In others, the
Church, as a body, adhered to its original confession ; but a majority of the parish or society,
which was the legal corporation associated
with the Church, declared the change of
basis, and voted to sustain a Unitarian minister.
Hence arose many disputes as to the possession
of church-property, and test cases were brought
before the civil courts for adjudication. Previ-
ously it had been loosely held in Massachusetts,
that churches themselves were bodies corporate, competent to hold property for the pur-

poses for which they are formed. But the Chief Justice now decided that " the only circumstance which gives a church any legal character is its connection with some regularly-constituted society." This decision largely favored the Unitarians ; and, as a consequence, not a few Orthodox *churches* (i.e., bodies spiritual) were dispossessed of their houses of worship by *congregations* (i.e., bodies corporate) which had become Unitarian. Still the court, though supposed to be biassed toward Unitarianism, decided the question, not upon disputed points of faith, but upon technical points of law.

In the year 1837, the General Assembly of the Presbyterian Church, representing that communion throughout the United States, by a summary vote of excision cut off whole presbyteries and synods for alleged errors in faith and discipline. The exscinded party at once organized a New General Assembly, with the same name as the Old ; and each body claimed to be *the* Presbyterian Church in the United States. The Assembly, as it existed before the division, held certain trust funds for educational

and benevolent purposes; and the " Old School,"
as they were called, remained in possession.
These funds being held by charter from the
State of Pennsylvania, the New-School Assembly brought a suit for the administration of the
same, or at least an equitable share in their
benefits; but the Supreme Court decided that
the title remained with the exscinding body.
Of course, the articles of faith and discipline
were considered in evidence, but only in the
point of view of legal construction. In 1870,
the two schools were re-united in one church.

Similar decisions in the State of New Jersey
are to the effect that " the courts cannot inquire
into the doctrines or opinions of any religious
society for the purpose of deciding whether
these are right or wrong ; but it is their duty to
do this when civil rights depend thereon, and
then it must be done by such evidence as the
nature of the case admits of."

In the State of Illinois, the controversy between Rev. Charles E. Cheney, rector of Christ
Church in Chicago, and Bishop Whitehouse,
the diocesan of the Episcopal Church in that
State, has led to several important decisions,

defining the position of the civil courts upon
ecclesiastical questions. From conscientious
scruples, Mr. Cheney was accustomed to omit
— as many Episcopal clergymen do — a phrase
in the baptismal service, as implying a false
doctrine of regeneration. For this liberty his
bishop called him to account before an ecclesiastical court, and, in accordance with its ver-
dict, forbade him to exercise the functions of a
minister in the Protestant Episcopal Church.
But the parish of Christ Church, through its
wardens, determined to stand by its rector; and
he has continued to officiate in that character.
To protect himself against the bishop, Mr. Cheney applied to the civil court for an injunction to
stay ecclesiastical proceedings, which threatened,
without cause, to deprive him of his livelihood,
and thus to interfere with his civil rights. The
court, however, decided, that, at this stage, the
case did not fall within its cognizance. But, on
the other hand, it is not possible for the bishop
to eject Mr. Cheney by any civil process, nor
to use a court of law to enforce in any way
the pains of his own ecclesiastical court.
Christ Church and Mr. Cheney could be

brought under the judicial power of the State only through an action brought by some member or members of the parish itself, upon the ground that the parish-property has been perverted from the true uses of an Episcopal church. That would be a question of fact for the courts to decide, as in any case of contract or usage, written or implied. Meantime Mr. Cheney's strength lies, not in the protection of any court, but in the determination of his parish to stand by him in his quarrel with his bishop. So long as the rights of person and property are not distinctly at issue, the State leaves the Church to settle such a quarrel in its own way.

Absolute uniformity in the ruling of the civil courts upon ecclesiastical questions in the different States is not to be looked for; but the principle universally obtains, that churches are known in law simply as corporations, and that no civil court can take cognizance of the doctrines, rules, usages, or actions, of a religious society, except so far as these relate to collateral questions affecting the disposal of property, or the civil rights of members of the body.

§ 4. *How Church Corporations are constituted.*
— The more usual method of constituting a
church corporation is through the medium of
trustees representing the local congregation.
For instance, in the State of New York, soon
after the Revolution, an act was passed " to
enable all the religious denominations in the
State to appoint trustees, who should be a body
corporate for the purpose of taking care of the
temporalities of their respective congregations,
and for other purposes therein mentioned "
(Act of April 6, 1784). This act has been
modified to suit the constitutions of different
churches. Thus, for the Episcopal Church,
the *vestry* of each particular congregation is,
" to all intents and purposes, a body corporate ; "
but the law prescribes the manner in which the
vestry shall be chosen. In the Reformed
Church, " the minister or ministers, and elders
or deacons, of every church or congregation "
(that is, the consistory), are made trustees, and a
body corporate. In the Methodist Church, " the
presiding elder and a majority of the district
stewards, appointed according to the discipline
of said church, for any given district," shall be

the body corporate for the church within that
district (Act of April 5, 1867). So long as
New York remained a Colony, the Roman-
Catholic Church was hardly able to gain a footing upon its soil. In July, 1700, it was enacted
that " every Jesuit and seminary priest, or
ecclesiastical person, made or ordained by any
authority derived, or pretended to be derived,
from the Pope or See of Rome, then residing
within the Province, should depart therefrom on
or before the 1st of November ensuing. Any
such person preaching, or teaching others to say
Popish prayers, masses, granting of absolution,
or celebrating or using any other of the Romish
ceremonies and rites of worship, shall be deemed
an incendiary and disturber of the public peace,
and an enemy to the true Christian religion."
Now, however, the Roman-Catholic is one of
the largest communions in the State, being
made up chiefly of Irish and German immigrants, and very largely of female servants.
For each congregation of the Roman-Catholic
Church, the archbishop or bishop of the diocese,
the vicar-general, the pastor of the particular
church, and two laymen, members of the same,

selected by the first three, are made trustees of the congregation. This provision betrays too great a concession on the part of politicians to the Roman-Catholic clergy. Nevertheless these Catholic trustees, just like the trustees of an insurance-company or a bank, " are required to exhibit upon oath to the Supreme Court in the judicial district in which each church is situated, and in every three years, an inventory of all the estate, real and personal, belonging to such church, and of the annual income thereof."

By the laws of the State of New York, every church is *restricted*, as to the amount of real and personal estate which it may hold, to a certain specified yearly income from the same; the design of this provision being to prevent the growth of rich and powerful ecclesiastical corporations. The three fundamental features of these laws are, —

1. Each particular church must be known to the law as a body corporate.

2. This body corporate must represent the lay element.

3. It must be restricted as to its annual revenue and income from real and personal estate.

Hence, by these principles, it is not legally possible for the Roman-Catholic Archbishop of New York, nor for the bishops collectively, to hold and control as a unit all the property of the Catholic Church within the State. Each individual congregation of that church — the congregation meeting in this or that village, or in this or that locality of a city, or under this or that specific name — must become a distinct corporation; and a certificate of that fact must be proved in the same manner as deeds of real estate, and filed in the office of the county clerk, and a copy in the office of the Secretary of State. The certificate runs as follows: " We the undersigned — to wit, A. B., the Roman-Catholic archbishop (or bishop) of the diocese of ——, C. D., vicar-general of such diocese, and E. F., pastor of the church of —— in such diocese, and —— laymen, members of the said church, duly selected and appointed — hereby certify that the name or title of —— is that by which they and their successors shall be known and distinguished as a body corporate, by virtue of the act of the legislature," &c. If the courts are true to their functions, the Roman-Catholic

Church in the United States can be held as closely as any corporation within the due restraints of law.

It is alleged that the Archbishop of New York evades the law concerning church-property by purchasing with church-funds property in his own name, and, at the same time, executing a quit-claim in blank form in favor of his successor. This quit-claim is held by the vicar-general : and, on the death of one archbishop, the name of the next archbishop is inserted in the deed ; and he, in like manner, executes a new quit-claim to insure the official succession to the property. Such an evasion of the law could not stand if it were fairly brought before the courts. In 1862, a citizen of New York bequeathed all his property " to the Right Rev. Bishop Hughes, in trust for the use and benefit of the Roman-Catholic Church of the State of New York." The bequest was declared void, on the ground that it was an attempt to create an express trust more extensive than was permitted by the statutes.

Yet experience has shown that it is well-nigh impossible to frame a law or to make a judicial

decision which the Roman-Catholic Church will
not evade, or pervert to its own advantage;
and in a city like New York, with a large proportion of Irish-Catholic voters, there are
always politicians who will court the priests
for the sake of their influence upon this pliant
body of electors. The Irish are clannish, and
follow enthusiastically their leaders; they are
credulous, and easily deceived by demagogues;
they are superstitious, and blindly obey their
priests : hence, where there is a large Roman-
Catholic constituency, it is easy for priests and
politicians to enter into collusion for the aggrandizement of the Roman-Catholic Church in
violation of the spirit of the laws. For instance, the act for the incorporation of Roman-
Catholic churches in New-York State provides
that the whole " real and personal estate of any
such church, exclusive of the church-edifice,
parsonage, and schoolhouses, together with the
land on which the same may be erected, shall
not exceed the annual income of three thousand dollars." But, under the pretext of
repairs, improvements, &c., many churches con-
trive to exceed this amount ; and besides, with

the connivance of politicians, the Catholic
churches obtain a release from assessments, and
also positive grants of large sums from the
State treasury, under the subterfuge of hospi-
tals, asylums, and various charities. Public attention has been roused to these abuses, and
they are likely to be corrected. But the Roman-Catholic Church never loses sight of its
own aggrandizement. In all times, under all
governments, through all professions and ap-
pearances, it is working ever toward one and
the same end ; and hence, while securing to
this subtle ecclesiastical organism the largest
religious freedom and the amplest protection of
the laws, American citizens keep up the watchword, "The price of liberty is eternal vigilance."

In the States of Massachusetts and Connecticut, the custom of raising money for the support of the Church by a tax levied upon the
town or parish prevailed for some time after the
Revolution ; but this has long since given place
to a system which has these substantial features :
The Church is regarded as a spiritual body,
made up of renewed souls (who have united

with it upon their own choice and confession);
and, as a body spiritual, it has no concern with
temporalities. But associated with each church
is a body of regular worshippers, who contribute
voluntarily toward its support. Under certain
regulations, these stated worshippers and con-
tributors are erected into a body corporate,
known as the parish, the congregation, or the
ecclesiastical society; and this body is known in
law, and holds the property of the church. In
many instances, however, the church itself, the
body spiritual, chooses also to become a body
corporate, and to act in both capacities. In
some of the new States of the West this is the
general custom.

§ 5. *No State Tax for Parish Dues.* — The old
idea of the parish as a territorial commune to
be taxed for the church has passed away; and
the ecclesiastical organization of a parish of the
Episcopal Church, for instance, gives to the
parish no civil or corporate powers. To obtain
such powers, the local church, or the parish or
society as its appointed representative, must
become a body corporate, each particular congregation under the law of the State in which

it is constituted. There can be no incorporation of any one church for the whole country.
Each particular congregation must provide
voluntarily for its own support by ways and
methods of its own. The simple form in common use in Massachusetts will serve to illustrate the working of this principle. It runs as
follows : " The undersigned, all of ——, in the
county of ——, in the Commonwealth of Massachusetts, do hereby associate ourselves together,
under the name of ——, as a parish or religious
society, at said —— ; and the purposes for
which this corporation is established are the
support of the public worship of God, and the
promotion of Christian knowledge and charity
according to the general usages of the ——
churches and parishes of Massachusetts." The
parish or society thus constituted elects its own
officers, frames its own laws (subject to general
statutes of the State), and enters into a compact
with the Church proper — the spiritual body
with which it is associated — concerning the
support of a pastor and other necessary provisions for church-worship ; and this compact is
valid and binding in law. Whatever the form

6

of adjustment, the law takes cognizance of a church only through its own act of incorporation as affecting the rights of property or of person : but should a church use its property in treasonable designs against the government, or for immoral or dangerous purposes, it would forfeit its corporate rights ; and no fiction of religious independence or liberty of conscience could cover such perversion and abuse. No church thus holding its right of corporate existence under American laws could be permitted to act contrary to those laws upon the plea of a paramount allegiance to a foreign sovereign.

# SECTION V.

## HOW CHURCHES ARE CONSTITUTED AND SUPPORTED.

§ 1. UNDER the laws of the United States, and of the several States of the Union, each church is at liberty to organize itself according to its own model, to frame its own laws, to raise its revenue in its own way, and to administer its own discipline. The broad principle is, that a church is a voluntary association; and its constitution, laws, and canons are stipulations between the parties, defining their duties and obligations. The civil rights of the members are still protected by the civil tribunals; but civil courts will not interfere to prevent an investigation before an ecclesiastical tribunal of a voluntary religious association when proceeding according to its constitution, canons, or rules, and when the subject-matter or person

is within its jurisdiction (Superior Court
of Chicago, 1863, — case of Hagar *vs.* Whitehouse).

The latest decision in the Cheney case at
Chicago, referred to in the preceding section,
defines these principles in the following
terms : —

" Where it appears that a local church and
the rector thereof are members of, and under
the supervision and control of, a general and
superior church organization, to whose faith
and discipline they have voluntarily attached
themselves, those who continue to adhere to the
faith and discipline of the general church are
the beneficiaries for whose use the trustees hold
the church-property, although they are the
minority of the local church organization.

" Where the proper ecclesiastical tribunals
have obtained jurisdiction, and have tried and
passed sentence of deposition upon an alleged
offender, civil courts not only recognize the
validity of, but give effect to, the decisions of
the church courts.

" In all matters of religious faith and practice,
the ecclesiastical courts, provided they have

obtained jurisdiction, are as entirely independent of the civil tribunals as the latter are of the former upon all questions relating to property interests.

" Neither will the courts, in absence of acts of incorporation which change the common law, permit a majority of the members of a church which is itself connected with and subject to the jurisdiction and government of a superior church judicatory to secede from the denomination to which they have voluntarily attached themselves, and take with them the church-property. Such an act is regarded in law as a perversion of the trust ; and a court of equity will reach forth its strong arm, and prevent it. The holders of the legal title are regarded in a court of equity as holding it in trust for the maintenance of the faith and worship of the founders of the organization ; and any diversion of it into another use is so far a breach of trust as to demand the interposition of the court. This position is sustained by many cases, English and American.

" The bill presents the case of a rector of the Protestant Episcopal Church, subject to its laws

and discipline, who has been regularly tried and
deposed by the proper church authority, but
who still continues to preach, and to be paid
therefor from the income of the church-property, and have the free use of the parsonage.
As a chancellor, I can now have nothing to do
with the regularity or irregularity, justice or
injustice, of that trial and deposition. I must,
for the purposes of this suit, accept it as a legal
procedure and judgment ; and, thus accepting it,
I must apply the law to the admitted facts of
the bill.

" The rule of law is, that a rightful sentence
of deposition precludes the deposed minister
from the right to occupy the pulpit, or administer divine ordinances, in the church to which
he is attached."

In other cases it has been decided that the
*majority* of a church had a right to change its
creed, and yet to retain the property ; but, in
this case, the Christ Church in Chicago still
claims to be an integral part of the Episcopal
Church.

If, however, a church should assume to
exercise civil powers and to administer civil

penalties, its action would at once be nullified
by the civil courts; and the claim of a church, or
of any religious body or order, to represent and
enforce the sovereignty of a foreign head in
contravention of the laws of a State or of the
Union, would not be tolerated for a moment.
Under the supreme sovereignty of the National
Constitution, each particular State of the Union
has a certain reserved and qualified sovereignty
within its own borders; but the notion of a
foreign sovereignty — as, for instance, at Rome
or at Mecca — over citizens of the United
States could not be allowed as a plea of religious obligation.

§ 2. *Churches Territorial, National, or Local.*
— In the United States, some ecclesiastical
organizations are, in their form, territorial or
national; and others are purely local and particular. Examples of the former are the
Episcopal, the Methodist, and the Presbyterian;
of the latter, the Baptist and the Congregational. By the theory of the *Episcopal* Church,
each State constitutes a diocese, or is sub-
divided into two or three dioceses, according to
its area and to the number of Episcopal com-

municants and congregations within its bounds.
Each diocese has its bishop; and the bishop
with the clergy of the diocese and a lay deputa-
tion form a *convention*, which meets annually for
the regulation of the affairs of the diocese.
Once in three years, a *general convention*, composed of all the bishops and of clerical and lay
delegates from each diocesan convention, meets
for the supreme direction of the Episcopal
Church in the whole country. This general
convention consists of a house of bishops, and
a house of clerical and lay deputies. But
each particular congregation of the Episcopal Church chooses its own rector, subject to
the approval of the bishop, and is incorporated
through its vestry, or other lay committee, for
the management of its own temporal affairs.
For the purpose of holding property, the Church
must conform in this respect to the local laws.

The *Methodist* Church divides the country
into districts or conferences. Each local conference, composed chiefly of the clergy and other
officials, appoints the ministers to the congregations within its bounds, changing them once
in every two or three years. There is no per-

manent pastorate, and the people have no voice in the selection of their ministers. A *general conference*, made up from all the local conferences, has absolute control over the Methodist Church in the whole country. But here, as before, the local laws must determine the mode of organization for holding property.

In the *Presbyterian* Church, each congregation is governed by a session, composed of the pastor and of lay elders chosen by the body of communicants in that particular congregation. The churches of a given district are combined in a *presbytery*, composed of their pastors and of an elder from each session. The presbytery has power of revision over the sessions within its bounds. Above the presbytery, and having a power of supervision over it, is the *synod*, comprehending a larger district, and made up of pastors and elders from all the congregations within its bounds. And above all these is the *general assembly*, made up of deputies from all the presbyteries, and having a final control over the whole Presbyterian Church in the United States. Thus all these churches, Episcopal, Methodist, Presbyterian, though having no connection with the State, and no support from the State, are in their structure territorial, and in their ideal national.

On the other hand, the Baptist and the Congregational churches are local and particular. Their theory is, that each assembly of Christian believers, united in a church covenant, and worshipping statedly together, is a church complete in itself, with power to appoint its own officers, and regulate its own affairs; that the government is vested solely in the *congregation of believers;* and that there can be no external jurisdiction over a particular church. These churches lay much stress upon the personal experience of regeneration, and a personal confession of faith, as conditions of church-membership; but these independent spiritual democracies establish fellowship with each other as co-ordinate bodies, and by voluntary methods maintain the communion of the churches. Upon the settlement of a pastor, or any occasion of special interest, a church invites the co-operation and sanction of the neighboring churches through a council convened for that specific object. These churches also meet together in conferences or conventions for spiritual improvement and for practical efficiency in Christian work. But such bodies have no power of ecclesiastical jurisdiction. Their influence is moral; but it carries with it the weight of collective wisdom and of acknowledged character.

The Congregational theory of the Church as a spiritual entity tends to conserve purity of faith and discipline. The parish system, as defined in the previous section, gives civil rights to the ecclesiastical corporation: the church covenant secures the purity of the spiritual body. This theory of the Church also enables Congregationalists to recognize as churches of Christ all communions of believers united in faith in Christ as their head, whatever their form of polity or of worship. In such a system there can be nothing despotic, nothing exclusive, nothing sectarian.* Moreover, by its simplicity, Congregationalism can work in harmony under any form of civil government. It asks

---

* As one example of the breadth of Christian liberty and unity in the Congregational polity, the author here presents a letter addressed to the renowned orator of Notre Dame in Paris, Père

only the right to be. Congregational churches
exist mainly in New England and at the West;
though, of late years, they have begun to multi-
ply in the Middle States, and even in the South.

§ 3. *Practical Working of the Free System.* —
One obvious tendency of the separation of the
churches from the State is to render the churches
more jealous for their own purity in faith and
in discipline. Each church or communion has

Hyacinthe, on his arrival in New York, after his famous protest
against the Vatican Council: —

Rev. FATHER HYACINTHE.

*Sir,* — Believing that many of your countrymen in New York would
be glad to hear the gospel at your eloquent lips, I am happy to place the
central and commodious church known as the Broadway Tabernacle at
your disposal for a preaching service in French on any Sunday after-
noon or evening. This invitation places the service under your direction, without condition or reservation. It is given as a tribute to your
Christian manliness and truth, and your fidelity as a preacher of the
gospel, and in the name of that catholicity which is above all divisions
of the Church, of that charity which is broader than names or nations,
of that liberty which you have so nobly illustrated and maintained, of
that truth which you have so fearlessly proclaimed; and, finally, in the
name of our Lord and Saviour Jesus Christ, who is the Supreme Head
of the Church Catholic and Universal.

Accept the assurances of my profound esteem.

JOSEPH P. THOMPSON, *Pastor.*

NEW YORK, Oct. 29, 1869.

To this Father Hyacinthe replied, that the delicacy of his relations to his own church rendered it inexpedient for him to exercise
his priestly functions at that time; but, should he preach at all in
New York, he would certainly accept an invitation so free and so
fraternal.

its own confession, and makes its own conditions of membership and rules of administration. The tendency is to draw the line sharply between " the Church " and " the world," and to consti- tute the Church according to the declaration of the Gospel of John : " As many as received him [i.e., as acknowledged Jesus to be the Christ], to them gave he power to become the sons of God, even to them that believe on his name , which were born, not of blood, nor of the will of the flesh, nor of the will of man, but of God " (John i. 12, 13). Though, in some churches, chil- dren baptized in infancy are confirmed and admit- ted to the Lord's supper at a suitable age, yet, as a rule, a personal confession of faith, and the experience and evidence of a renewed heart, are required for admission to the full privileges of church-membership. Hence, in reading the sta- tistics of the American churches, it should be borne in mind that the term *members* by no means represents the total of worshippers in the several congregations, or of nominal adherents to a con- fession, but only those who by their own act have united with the church proper, the spiritual body, and who partake of its sacraments. These are commonly called " communicants."

The Roman-Catholic Church reports as members all persons who are born and baptized within its pale. The Protestant churches do not report as members the children of communicants (though these have been baptized), but only those who by their own avowal of faith have become communicants. Hence the reported number of church-members falls very far short of the whole Protestant population, and also of the actual number who attend upon divine worship, and who contribute to the support of the churches. The efficient spiritual membership of the five leading Protestant communions in 1872 was as follows: —

|                    | Church Organizations. | Communicants. |
|--------------------|:---------------------:|:-------------:|
| Baptists,          | 18,397                | 1,489,191     |
| Congregationalists,| 3,202                 | 312,054       |
| Episcopalians,     | 2,835                 | 239,218       |
| Methodists,        | 25,278                | 2,047,876     |
| Presbyterians,     | 6,275                 | 559,372       |
|                    | 55,987                | 4,647,711     |

To these five leading communions should be added, for the Lutheran, the Reformed, the Moravian, and other smaller bodies, about 12,000 church organizations, and 1,500,000 communicants; giving a grand total of 68 000 Protestant

churches, with upwards of 6,000,000 communicants. But the number of persons who habitu-
ally attend the worship of these churches is
probably 15,000,000 ; for, on an average, from
sixty to seventy per cent of the stated members
of a congregation are not church-communicants.
The Protestant population of the United States
is computed at more than 30,000,000.

Each church or communion makes its own
rules for the ordination of ministers, the admission of members, and the enforcement of discipline ; and since the communicants enter the
body of their own free will, and can withdraw
from it at their pleasure, without thereby affecting any civil right, the sternness of a church-
creed or the strictness of church-discipline is a
matter with which neither the State nor the
public has any concern.

Those who like an iron-bound, ecclesiastical
organization, can enter it : those who do not
can let it alone, and can provide for themselves
a church more liberal in faith and practice.

Yet both public opinion and the courts would
interfere to protect the personal and civil
rights of citizens if these were threatened by

measures of church-discipline.  A member of
a church who had been excommunicated upon
a charge of adultery, believed to be sustained,
yet lacking such technical evidence as would
satisfy a jury, brought a suit against the pastor for giving public notice of the excommunication, as an act of slander injuring his standing in the community.  The court held, that,
in a case of public scandal affecting the purity of a church, the church was entitled to an
open vindication ; but, nevertheless, due caution
must be used not to injure the good name of an
individual by hasty or prejudiced proceedings.

Recently a citizen of Kalamazoo, Mich., lent
a priest a sum of money to help build a parish,
which the Catholic bishop refused to recognize
subsequently as a loan.  The poor man, fearing
a foreclosure of the mortgage on his farm,
brought suit in chancery against the bishop.
For doing this he was forbidden to partake of
the communion by the bishop during the episcopal visit; and the edict of excommunication was
read to him.  Fearfully frightened, he asked
what his offence had been, and was told that he
was excommunicated for having sued a bishop

of the church. Being a devout believer in the
powers of the clergy, he was frightened nearly
out of his wits, and implored the bishop to re-
voke the excommunication. This was done on
condition that he would withdraw his suit. He
complied with the demand; and the interdict
was removed. It was too late, however; and
the wretched man sank beneath the weight of
his fancied guilt, and died. The matter created
much excitement in Michigan; and a bill was at
once introduced into the legislature punishing by
a fine of from one to five thousand dollars, or imprisonment from one to five years, any bishop
or priest who shall excommunicate, or threaten
to excommunicate, any member, to prevent him
from commencing any suit or collecting any claim.

The multiplicity of sects growing out of the
spirit of freedom is thought by some to be an
evil result of the separation of the Church from
the State; * but this is an instance where division upon subordinate points tends to a higher

* Dr. Döllinger of Munich, leader of the " Old Catholic " movement, when urged by the author to attend the Evangelical Alliance
in New York, replied, " What could I hope to do for Christian union
in a country where you make a new sect every day? "

unity in substantial principles. In religion, as in every thing else, the American people carry out the noble sentiment of William Penn, the founder of the Quaker Colony of Pennsylvania: " We must give the liberty we ask." In civil affairs, the best guaranty for my liberty is that an equal liberty is accorded to every other man ; and my freedom of conscience is made perfect when to every man is secured the liberty of believing or of not believing, of worshipping or of not worshipping, as he will. I should be as jealous for my neighbor's rights as for my own.

Now, this habit of respecting one another's rights cherishes a feeling of mutual respect and courtesy. If, on the one hand, the spirit of independence fosters individualism, on the other it favors good-fellowship. All sects are equal before the law. The State does not sustain any one or two or ten, but leaves all equally free to consult their own welfare. In our homely proverb, " Every tub must stand on its own bottom." Hence one great cause of jealousy and distrust is removed ; and though, at times, sectarian zeal may lead to rivalries and controversies unfavorable to unity, on the other hand the independence and equality of the churches favor their voluntary co-operation; and in no country is the practical union of Christians more beautifully or more beneficially exemplified than in the United States. With the exception of the Roman Catholics, Christians of all communions are accustomed to work together in the spirit of mutual concession and confidence, in educational, missionary, and philanthropic measures for the general good. The motto of the State holds of the Church also, — *E pluribus unum*. As a rule, a bigoted church or a fierce sectarian is despised.

Each local church defrays its expenses by some method of voluntary support on the part of its own attendants. In some churches, especially among the Methodists, all the sittings are free; and each member makes a weekly, monthly, or quarterly subscription toward defraying current expenses. But the common method of raising church-revenue is by the rent of pews; each pew being adapted for a family, and containing from four to six sittings. Sometimes pews are sold to individual members of the congregation to defray the original cost of the church-building, and then are subjected to a yearly tax. Thus in New York, where the expense of building and supporting a church is great, it is no unusual thing for a man to pay from one thousand to three thousand dollars for a pew, to be held in his own right, and a yearly tax of eight or ten per cent upon this cost. In other cases, the cost of the edifice is met by liberal subscriptions; the building is dedicated to God as a thank-offering, free of debt, and with no private ownership; and the pews are rented by the year or the quarter to meet current expenses. Usually the churches are fitted up with carpets, cushions, and every comfort and convenience to render them homelike and attractive; especially are they well warmed, well lighted, well cleaned, and well ventilated.

The Broadway Tabernacle Church, with which the author was connected for more than twenty-five years, upon the completion of a new house of worship had a debt of sixty-five thousand dollars. In one year, twenty-five thousand dollars of this debt was paid off by free gifts, in addition to the cost of maintaining public worship; and in the following year the

remaining forty thousand dollars was paid off
by a subscription made by the congregation at
one single Sunday service. The yearly income
from pew-rents was about eighteen thousand dollars.* The great popularity of Mr. Beecher (a
brother of Mrs. Stowe) in Brooklyn creates
such a competition for sittings in Plymouth
Church, that the pews are put up at auction
every year, and yield a revenue of more than
fifty thousand dollars. This, of course, is an
exceptional case; but in many city churches
the yearly revenue from pew-rents ranges from
ten thousand to thirty thousand dollars, and
the pews are rated from fifty up to four hundred
dollars a year. These sums are cheerfully paid.
The same method prevails in smaller towns and

---

* In the course of twenty-five years, the Broadway Tabernacle
Church raised by pew-rents and subscriptions, for erecting the
church edifice and sustaining its own worship, the round sum of
four hundred thousand dollars; and in the same period it contributed for home and foreign missions, theological seminaries, and
other religious objects, the round sum of three hundred and fifty
thousand dollars; a total of seven hundred and fifty thousand dollars
from an average congregation of a thousand persons, many of
whom possessed little property. The salary of the pastor was advanced, with the rates of living, from two thousand to nine thousand dollars a year.

in country villages; but the rates are much
lower, the pew-rents being graduated by the
current expenses.

The advantages of this system are, that it
secures the personal interest of the members in
their particular church, and that it makes the
church a family institution. Families that go
always to the same church, and sit together in
the same pew, regard the church as a *home;* and
children grow up with this home-attachment to
the house of God. The disadvantage of this
pew-system is, that it tends to the exclusion of
the poor, and not of the poor only, but of persons of moderate income, who cannot meet
these large demands for the expenses of public
worship in the great cities. To obviate this
evil, some churches have sittings graduated according to the means of different classes of
worshippers; others provide free sittings for the
poor, or declare the galleries always free to
strangers, or hold one service every Sunday at
which all the seats are free to all comers. As a
rule, every church recognizes its obligation to
provide the preaching of the gospel for the
masses of the community. Hence the number

of church-members; that is, persons who by
their own free act have joined the spiritual
body, in distinction from the society or parish.
This number of *communicants* by no means
represents the popular interest in religion.    In
the United States, as a rule, it is respectable to
be religious; and, in smaller communities, it
favors one's social standing if he goes regularly
to church.    Père Hyacinthe of Paris, after a
journey in the New-England States, said that
three institutions seemed to mark an American town, and to be all equally dear to the
people, — the bank, the school, and the
church.

It would be a most serious error to infer, from
the relatively small number of actual communicants, that the majority of the population are
irreligious or indifferent, and that the poor are
abandoned to heathenism.    There are multitudes of truly devout and godly persons who do
not take upon themselves the responsibility of
active church-membership; and there is a still
greater number of non-communicants, who show
a decent outward respect for religion without
making a profession of piety.    Upon festive

occasions, and even at political conventions, it is quite common to request a clergyman to officiate as a chaplain of the assembly. In times of sickness or domestic sorrow, almost all families seek the consolations of religion. Almost all sufferers and mourners welcome the visit of a clergyman, though at other times they may seldom enter a church. Though marriage is a civil contract, almost every one prefers to hallow it by the sanctions of religion; and a burial without a religious service is so infrequent as to be regarded almost as a mark of heathenism. Religion is most honored where it is least enforced.

In all great cities, systematic provision is made for the religious welfare of the poor. The experiment of "free churches" built for their special use has failed, because the pride of even the humblest American rebels against advertising his poverty and accepting a gratuity. The native American servant never asks for *trinkgeld*, and would feel insulted if this were offered him for every petty service; and the commonest laborer would resent being branded as a beggar in his religion. But mission-schools and mission-churches are established in the midst of the quarters of the poor. These are sustained chiefly by wealthy churches, or by mission-societies; but the poorest worshipper is encouraged to give something to the church as an act of self-respect and a token of proprietorship in the services. The mission-churches are neat and inviting, and have connected with them industrial schools. Systematic visitation is conducted for the relief of want; and religion is presented with the hand of sympathy and the heart of love. In the great cities, each large church has schools and missions of its own; and churches of all confessions combine to canvass every district, and to supply every family with the means of grace.

For the propagation of religion in the country new churches are built by the voluntary subscriptions of their members, aided, perhaps, by older churches of the same communion, or by societies which exist for this purpose. Such a society will agree to give so much toward building a church, or supporting its pastor, on condition that the church shall raise a certain specified amount within a given time.

For example, the Baptist Mission Society has raised a fund of half a million dollars, the income of which is to be expended in loans, without interest, to aid in building churches in new sections of the country. There are now a hundred and eleven churches in twenty-four different States holding loans from this fund. In 1872 it aided in building fifty-three churches. The Congregational Church-Building Society aids about an equal number of churches yearly, not, however, by a loan, but by a free grant, upon condition that the congregation thus assisted will complete the house of worship free from debt. Other communions have modifications of the same system; and every church thus aided in its infancy becomes, in turn, a helper of others.

§ 4. *Financial Results of the Voluntary System.* — In 1837, Washington Irving, in one of his sketches, to satirize the money-getting propensity of his countrymen, represented " the almighty dollar " as the chief divinity of the American people. This witty phrase has been caught at by foreigners as expressing the one

universal national characteristic of Americans.
Daniel's Geography gives it as a satirical exag-
geration : " Der Handelsgeist der ernsten, beson-
nenen und kalten Americaner artet oft in eine so
unverhohlene Ueberschätzung des Mammons
aus, dass wohl Spötter mit Uebertreibung be-
merkt haben : trots ihrer strengen Religiosität
sei ihr eigentlicher Golt der Dollar." * It is
true that the people of the United States have
shown an almost unprecedented energy in
the development of material resources, and
have risen rapidly both in individual and in
national wealth. This was due, in part, to the
necessity of their condition. Their first task
was to subdue the continent for the occupation
of civilized man ; and the whole world now
reaps the benefit of American utilitarianism.
The needy and the adventurous from all nations
rush to America to share its spoils ; and the
scholars and artists of the Old World have not
shown themselves averse to the American dollar. As Lowell has wittily said, " All, without
exception, make no secret of regarding us as

---

* Lehrbuch der Geographie, von Prof. Dr. H. A. Daniel. 32 unver-
änderte Auflage, herausgegeben von Dr. A. Kirchhoff, p. 150.

the goose bound to deliver them a golden egg in return for *their* cackle." * But, as he reminds us, "Human nature has a much greater genius for sameness than for originality;" and, now that Germany has suddenly the opportunity of rapid wealth, one hears in Berlin quite as much talk of prices, rents, losses, and gains, and sees quite as much eagerness for material prosperity, even at the expense of the ideal life, as in New York itself. Even palaces are sold for new streets of building-lots. Meantime the Americans are more and more subjecting the material to the ideal. If heretofore they have worshipped the dollar, they have burnt their fingers in sacrificing to that Moloch, and have learned to consecrate the dollar to the noblest uses of humanity.

From the very first, there was in America an ideal life. Schools were planted, and learning was cherished, from the beginning. Intellectual culture and spiritual refinement have been the characteristics of New England; and, with the growth of wealth, the Americans have not forgotten to cherish letters, science, and art, until

* My Study Windows.

now museums of science founded by private munificence will compare favorably with those of the Old World, and American libraries and galleries purchase the treasures which impoverished nobles of France and Italy are willing to exchange for the almighty dollar. There exists in American society a guild of the cultivated, to which no money could purchase admission.

From the first, religion has trained the American people to believe that the dollar should be consecrated to God and to humanity. Yet, " till after our civil war, it never seemed to enter the head of any foreigner, especially of any Englishman, that an American had what could be called a country, except as a place to eat, sleep, and trade in. Then it seemed to strike them suddenly : ' By Jove, you know, fellahs don't fight like that for a shop-till.' To Americans America is something more than a promise and an expectation. It has a past and traditions of its own. A descent from men who sacrificed every thing, and came hither, not to better their fortunes, but to plant their idea in virgin soil, should be a good pedigree. There was never colony, save this, that went forth, not to seek gold, but God." *

Americans are quite as much addicted to the worship of the heroic and the ideal as to the worship of the dollar. For the memory of the past, for the ideals of law and liberty, they sacrificed three hundred thousand lives, and three thousand millions of dollars; and now they have taxed "the almighty dollar" to reduce this debt by four hundred millions in four years. And in the same period they have contributed more than any nation of Europe, by voluntary gifts, for the promotion of science and art and the advancement of religion.

England most nearly approaches the United States in private munificence for learning, religion, and charity; and in England a like spirit of freedom is found under somewhat different forms.

In the year 1872, the five leading denominations in the United States raised for their church-expenses, for home and foreign missions, for theological institutes, &c., the following sums:—

---

* Lowell: My Study Windows, p. 75.

| | |
|---|---|
| The Baptists, | $3,391,276 |
| The Congregationalists, about | 4,000,000 |
| The Episcopalians, | 6,304,608 |
| The Methodists, | 17,427,184 |
| The Presbyterians, | 11,070,325 |

(The Presbyterians raised, in 1870, over eight million ; in 1871, over nine million.)

Add to these the Lutherans, the Reformed, and other communions, and the sum expended for religious uses by the whole body of Protestant churches in 1872 was at least fifty million dollars. The property held by these churches, the most of it originally purchased by the contributions of their membership, is valued at nearly three hundred million dollars. Such are some of the fruits of voluntary religion in the United States. A people who would enjoy the luxury of perfect religious liberty must relinquish all church-aid from the State or the Commune, and be willing to pay out of their own pockets the full cost of maintaining the church of their choice. When once they have learned to do this, they will love to do it.

## SECTION VI.

### INCIDENTAL RELATIONS OF THE STATE TO RELIGION.

§ 1. It has been held by English courts that Christianity is a part of the common law of the land; but the attempt to establish the same doctrine in the United States has been over-ruled by the highest judicial authority. Some years ago, Mr. Stephen Girard bequeathed to the city of Philadelphia lands and money for the establishment of a college for orphans, upon the condition that no minister of any religion should ever be admitted within its walls, and no tenets of any sect should be taught to the pupils. The heirs-at-law of Mr. Girard attempted to set aside this will; and Mr. Daniel Webster, familiarly called the " Expounder of the Constitution," argued, on their behalf, that Christianity was a part of the common law, and therefore the attempt of the testator to exclude the Christian religion from his college was illegal, and the bequest was void. But the decisions of the courts upon this and parallel cases involving the same principle were to this effect; viz., "Though certain features of the common law may have been derived from the Christian religion, the law does not attempt to enforce the precepts of Christianity on the ground of their sacred character or divine origin. Christianity is not a part of the law of the land in the sense that would entitle the courts to take notice of and base their judgments upon it, except so far as they should find that its precepts had been incorporated in, and thus become a component part of, the law." (See Vidal *vs.* Girard Executors, 2 How. 198; Andrew *vs.* Bible Society, 4 Sandford, 182; and Cooley, "Constitutional Limitations," p. 472.) The recent proposal to amend the Constitution by a declaration that the Christian religion is the obligatory rule of national life does not meet with much favor from the clergy or from the religious press.

§ 2. *The Oath.* — The Constitution of the

United States requires that the President, before entering upon the execution of his office, shall take the following oath or affirmation: " I do solemnly swear (or affirm) that I will faithfully execute the office of President of the United States; and will, to the best of my ability, preserve, protect, and defend the Constitution of the United States " (Art. II., sect. 1, § 9). Art. VI., sect. 3, provides, also, that the senators and representatives of the National Congress, and the members of the several State legislatures, and all executive and judicial officers both of the United States and of the several States, " shall be bound by oath or affirmation to support this Constitution." It will be seen from the form of the oath prescribed to the President that no religious ceremonies or sanctions are attached to this solemnity; but a simple affirmation, such as a Quaker might make, would meet the requirements of the case. In some of the States, however, it is required of a witness, before taking an oath, that he shall declare his belief in the existence of God, and in a state of rewards and punishments after the present life. This is the old principle of the common law; but several States have expressly abolished this declaration of religious belief as preliminary to the taking of an oath. The real question in the case does not concern the faith of the witness, but his veracity or trustworthiness; and the immediate fear of imprisonment for perjury may be more salutary than the remote fear of punishment in a future state.

§ 3. *Religious Days.* — The Constitution of the United States contains an indirect recognition of Sunday as a *dies non*. It is in these words: "If any bill shall not be returned by the President within ten days (*Sundays excepted*) after it shall have been presented to him, the same shall be a law in like manner as if he had signed it." In some of the States there are stringent Sunday laws, which prohibit secular employments upon that day, and impose various restrictions upon public amusements. Such laws are, for the most part, a tradition of the old Puritan sabbath, which, with all its formal and doctrinal strictness, has had much to do with the development of that moral manhood for which New

England especially has been distinguished. In their re-action against mere "commandments and traditions of men," as these were enforced in the Romish Church, the Puritans so magnified the authority of the Bible as to make it the rule of practice for the citizen, as well as the rule of faith for the Christian. Rejecting the saints' days and other sacred days imposed by ecclesiastical authority, they revived the Jewish sanctity of the sabbath, and enacted the fourth commandment into a series of laws, which forbade work, travel, pleasure, on the Lord's Day, and even required attendance at church.* In all this the motive was good, but

---

* Some European writers on America have been misled by a book, published in London in 1781, giving the so-called "Blue Laws" of New Haven: "No one shall travel, cook victuals, make beds, sweep house, cut hair, or shave, on the sabbath day. No woman shall kiss her child on the sabbath or fasting day. No one shall read Common Prayer, keep Christmas or saint days, make minced pies, dance, play cards, or play on any instrument of music except the drum, trumpet, and jew's-harp. Every male shall have his hair cut round according to a cap." These "Blue Laws" are a pure fiction. No trace of such rules, nor of any thing like them, can be found in the legislation of the Colony. Just before the war of Independence, one Samuel Peters, a notorious liar, made himself so obnoxious as a royalist, that he was obliged to flee; and he took his revenge by publishing in England a fictitious satire upon the Puritans.

the policy was mistaken. As Froude has said, "When nations can grow to maturity in a single generation, when the child can rise from his first grammar-lesson a matured philosopher, individual men may clear themselves by a single effort from mistakes which are embedded in the heart of their age." Of late years, however, the tendency has been to modify or repeal all special Sunday laws, or to allow them to become a dead letter. So far as they have been tested before the courts, they have been defended mainly upon two grounds, — the right of the citizen to the quiet and peaceable enjoyment of public worship in the exercise of his religious liberty ; and the expediency, upon sanitary and moral grounds, of a weekly cessation from labor, with a suitable restriction upon temptations to vice.

For a like reason, as a precaution against drunkenness and riotous behavior, the laws provide, that, on election-days and holidays, places where intoxicating drinks are sold shall be closed. Sunday laws and sumptuary laws are often criticised and ridiculed as a peculiarity of " Puritan " New England ; but, before the set-

tlement of Massachusetts, in Virginia, where
the Church of England was established, every
colonist was obliged to attend church twice
every Sunday, "upon pain, for the first fault, to
lose their provision and allowance for the whole
week following; for the second, to lose said
allowance, and also to be whipped; and, for the
third, to suffer death." (Hening, Statutes at
Large, i. 123, 144, 261. See in Palfrey,
"History of New England," ii. 34.) Such
legislation was borrowed from English pre-
cedents, and long ago passed from American
statute-books. The intent of existing Sunday
laws in America is not to coerce conscience, nor
to enforce worship, but to secure order and
decorum upon the stated religious holiday.
Such laws, however, derive their force chiefly
from the prevailing public sentiment, and are
an attempt to embody in legislation the average
moral sense of the community. As has been
said in the previous section, American society
is largely pervaded by the sentiment of defer-
ence to religion. It is respectable to be religious, or at least to show a respect for religion.
The wealthy and cultivated classes are accus-

tomed to attend church. The leading men of the
community are often communicants. Hence
the custom of opening the sessions of Congress
and of the State legislatures with prayer, of
appointing chaplains to the army and the navy,
and of designating by public authority days of
thanksgiving * and of fasting, has the sanction
of public opinion, and is not looked upon as an
intrusion by the State into the domain of religious freedom. When New-Year's Day, Washington's Birthday, the Fourth of July, or any
other festival, falls upon a Sunday, the following
Monday is observed as the holiday; and the
sabbath is kept with religious quiet as usual.
In many States, houses of religious worship are
exempted from taxation for the support of the
civil government, upon the ground that religion,
as a conservator of public morals, assists in pre-
serving the peace and order of society (see
in Cooley, p. 471).

§ 4. *Jealousy of Ecclesiastics.* — Upon the
other hand, some of the State constitutions
make the ministers of any religion ineligible to
civil office by reason of their ecclesiastical

* Appendix I.

functions. This proscription of the clergy as a class was probably due to that jealousy of ecclesiastical meddling in civil affairs which the Jesuits had already awakened in some of the infant Colonies, and which passed over by tradition to some even of the newer States. The tendency of the Roman-Catholic Church, from its very organization, is to constitute an *imperium in imperio;* and it may yet become in the United States an organic power of perpetual revolution against the State. Hence some American patriots have contended that Roman Catholics should be excluded from office, and even from the polls, because history had shown their church to be inimical to liberty. Twenty years ago, a political party was formed, with the secret watchword "Know-Nothing," for the purpose of shutting out Catholics from political privileges; but, as soon as its purpose was known, the party was discarded by the good sense of the people and their love of fair play. We cannot forget, that, in English history, Puritans and evangelical reformers were treated as enemies of the State; and that the power of political proscription for religious opinions is a two-edged sword, and might be turned by the dominant party against any class of citizens. So was it, in fact, in the reigns of Henry VIII. and of Queen Elizabeth in England.

Moreover, United-States law is wisely jealous of "constructive treason;" and the National Constitution expressly declares that "treason against the United States shall consist only in levying war against them, or in adhering to their enemies, giving them aid and comfort." It would be contrary to the whole spirit of American institutions to proscribe Roman Catholics as a class, or their clergy, or any order within their church, simply upon suspicion of political intrigue; but if found guilty of conspiring against the government, either as individuals or as a society, they could be dealt with, not as Catholics, but as rebels or traitors. A secret order in the Southern States, known as the Ku-Klux, which was conspiring against the government, has been outlawed, and its members punished by court-martial. Had they claimed to be a religious order, acting for the " higher interests " of the Church, this could not have shielded them from punishment as conspirators.

The discrimination against the clergy as a class, in some of the State constitutions, is an anomaly as contrary to the spirit of religious liberty as would be the erection of an Established Church. The State of New York has abolished this feature, which marred its early constitution. As a rule, clergymen decline political honors; though some have been members of Congress and of various State legislatures, and have held offices in the civil service of the United States. As a body, they have been eminently loyal and patriotic; and, in times of public peril, they have rendered efficient service to the country.*

---

* The following example, of which the author was an eye-witness, will illustrate how ministers and churches in America uphold the government, without seeking for themselves any favor from the State. The Broadway Tabernacle Church (Congregational) in New York has already been mentioned. From this congregation five and twenty young men voluntarily enlisted in the army. Five of these died in the service, of whom two were brought home to be buried lovingly from the bosom of the church. The Sanitary, Christian, and Union Commissions had its constant and energetic support. The great fairs were largely officered and equipped from the women of this congregation. By solemn vote and prayer they sent

The pulpit in the United States has ever been among the foremost of social forces, stimulating the people to intellectual life, encouraging cul-

their pastor to minister upon the battle-fields of Tennessee: they greeted his return with fresh outpourings of bounty for the soldiers. Again and again they draped organ and pulpit with flags, and made the church a rallying-ground for Liberty and Union under the uplifted banner of the cross; and, when all was over, they held a majestic requiem for three hundred thousand dead.

But there was one incident of the war which signalized the loyal devotion of this church to the country and to Christ. It was in that darkest hour when delays and defeats had so blighted hope, that treason came out from its lurking-places in the North, and hissed its venom at the government; when the President hesitated either to enforce the draft or to call for volunteers; and when timid conservatives began to say, "We had better give it up, and make terms." The pastor came into the pulpit with a plea for Christian manhood, saying, "Of what avail are our churches if we shall no longer have a government or a country? Of what worth is our Christianity if it cannot preserve these? If the government cannot save the country, let the churches save both. Let this church call for volunteers; equip a regiment, and put it into the field, to show that *we* will never give it up." At the close of the service, some one called upon the congregation to remain; proposed a subscription for a church regiment; and, before night of that memorable sabbath, upwards of thirty thousand dollars were laid upon the altar. Two women sent each five hundred dollars, saying, "We cannot go: put men in our stead." That action went like a flash of electricity through the land. It brought letters of thanks from senators at Washington, from members of the cabinet, from generals in the field. It cheered the burdened heart of the President, and gave new courage to his indomitable Minister of War.

ture and science, and creating a public sentiment outside of the Church itself for all that is
true and noble and good. The ministry attracts
to it a large percentage of the best minds of
the country. The training for the pastoral
office, in most denominations, is thorough and
severe. As a rule, when a boy has pursued the
common-school education till thirteen or four-
teen, he enters a classical academy, where he
remains for three years in special preparation
for college. In this time he studies Sallust,
Cæsar, Cicero, Virgil, Xenophon's " Anabasis,"
Homer's " Iliad," arithmetic, algebra, geometry,
grammar, geography, &c.; and he must pass a
strict examination in these branches in order to
be admitted to college. Next he spends four
years in college, where he studies, in Latin, Livy,
Horace, Cicero, Juvenal, Plautus, Tacitus; in
Greek, Homer, Herodotus, Æschylus, Sopho-
cles, Plato, Demosthenes, Thucydides ; in math-
ematics, geometry, trigonometry, conic sections,
differential and integral calculus, physics, me-
chanics, astronomy; also the French and German languages, comparative philology, rhetoric,
logic, history (Grecian, Roman, Mediæval, and

English), mental philosophy, political economy and philosophy, chemistry, anatomy, physiology, geology, botany. These studies are, for the most part, obligatory, and are tested by rigid examinations. The college is the academic faculty of the university; and, after this course of four years in general culture, the candidate for the ministry passes under the special faculty for theology. Here he remains for three years longer in the study of Hebrew grammar and philology, Greek exegesis, dogmatic, symbolic, natural theology, church history, church polity, Christian literature, sacred rhetoric and homiletics, and pastoral theology. In the theological faculty, all lectures are free; and the students are provided with comfortable rooms, text-books, &c., free of charge. Large sums are given by the churches for the education of the clergy. A learned ministry is the strength of religion in America.

§ 5. *The State and Morality.* — The State is, in its own nature, both *jural and ethical*. It is grounded in moral reasons, and exists for moral ends. Hence it has authority to suppress vice and crime, and whatever outrages morality and decency. The plea of conscience or of religious liberty cannot be used to cover offences against the moral sense of the community, or against the peace and order of the family and of society. The Supreme Court of Ohio has ruled that " acts evil in their nature, or dangerous to the public welfare, may be forbidden and punished, though sanctioned by one religion, and prohibited by another: but this creates no preference whatever; for they would be equally forbidden and punished if all religions permitted them. Thus no plea of religion could shield a murderer, a ravisher, or a bigamist; for the community would be at the mercy of superstition if such crimes as these could be committed with impunity because sanctioned by some religious delusion " (Bloom *vs.* Richards, 2 Ohio State Reports, 390, 391). It is upon this ground, as was shown in the first section, that the State can deal with bigamy and polygamy as offences against the well-being of society ; though the Mormons have sought to cover them with the sanctions of religion.

The ethics of society control the legislation of the United States upon adultery, bigamy, drunkenness, indecency, and like social vices affecting the public morality. All such offences are dealt with by the State as a moral and ethical *being* having charge of the welfare of society. Immoral exhibitions, actions, and publications are by law suppressed in the United States more rigorously and effectively than in most countries of Europe : * for the conviction that underlies all moral and ethical legislation is, that the safeguards of freedom are intelligence and virtue ; that since intemperance and immorality cast upon society the burdens of pauperism, of disease, of illegitimacy, impair the fitness of the citizen for his duties as an elector, and demoralize the community, therefore, as a measure of self-protection, the State,

---

* A bill to prevent the mailing of obscene books, papers, articles, and advertisements, has passed Congress, and been signed by the President. The person who " knowingly deposits, or causes to be deposited, for mailing or delivery," obscene articles, publications, or advertisements, in the post-office, and the person who, "in pursuance of any plan or scheme for disposing " of any of the indecent books or articles advertised, takes them from the mails, are alike deemed guilty of a high misdemeanor, and, on conviction, shall be fined from a hundred to five thousand dollars, with costs; or imprisoned at hard labor from one to ten years, or both, in the discretion of the court.

as a corporate being, whose very existence implies jural and ethical functions, can and must
put forth its power to sustain good morals,
and thus to preserve a free political society.

A very large percentage of vice and crime
in the United States, especially in the great
cities, is chargeable to European immigration.
The police statistics of New York show that
the vast majority of persons arrested for criminal offences are of European birth; and of
these, again, the great majority are natives of
Ireland.* Thus, reared under the European

---

* Of 80,532 persons arrested by the police of New York in 1867,
only 27,156 were of American birth; and, of the 53,376 foreigners
who disturbed the peace of the city, 38,128 were Irish.  From 1860
to 1868, there were, within the precincts of the New-York metropoli-
tan police, 706,288 arrests.  Of these there were 204,129 Americans;
the foreigners numbering 502,159, of which 373,341 were Irish.
This preponderance of foreign-born criminals is not peculiar to New
York, where, naturally, the worst elements of immigration would
remain.  The same ratio appears in the country at large.

The following facts are authentic.  In prison in the United States,
on June 1, 1871, there were 32,901 persons, thus distributed: —

| | |
|---|---|
| Total prisoners | 32,901 |
| Native whites | 16,117 |
| Colored people | 8,056 |
| Foreign born | 8,728 |
| Total population | 38,558,371 |
| Native white population | 28,111,133 |
| Colored population | 4,880,009 |
| Foreign-born population | 5,567,229 |

system of *State* religions, persons baptized, taught, and confirmed in State churches, or, as in Ireland, reared under the imperious ecclesiastical authority of Rome, become the outlaws of American society. America owes to Europe those two deadly foes of evangelical religion, Romanism and Rationalism; while Mormonism is recruited almost entirely from Northern Europe. Hence the feeling is quite prevalent in the United States, that a system of *State* religion tends toward a practical heathenism and unbelief; that its training tends to substitute forms and dogmas for a personal religious faith, and its restraints and compulsions tend to produce a re-action against all belief: while the free religious system of the United States develops in

Showing that (assuming all in prison to be criminals) there is, at least, one criminal in every 1,172 of the population, one in every 1,744 of our native white population, one in every 637 of our foreign-born population, and one in every 605 of our colored population.

When European journals picture crime as abounding in the United States, they should have the candor to add, that, though foreigners compose only one-sixth of the total white population, they furnish one-third of the white criminals, and, in the ratio of criminals, are on a level with the ignorant and degraded negroes. Their crimes are not a fruit of American society.

church-members the sense of personal responsibility and the spirit of religious activity; and the exhibition of these commands the respect of the community for religion, and infuses into society a healthy moral sentiment, which, in turn, sustains the State in enforcing essential morality by the authority of law. De Tocqueville was profoundly impressed with this feature of American society. He said, " Religion in America takes no direct part in the government of society : but it must be regarded as the first of their political institutions; for, if it does not impart a taste for freedom, it facilitates the use of it. Thus, whilst the law permits the Americans to do what they please, religion prevents them from conceiving, and forbids them to commit, what is rash or unjust." — *Democracy in America*, chap. xvii.

§ 6. *The State and Education.* — Most of the States make provision in their constitutions for a system of free public education. This was the first care of the New-England Puritans ; and the Congress of the United States has aided this system by large grants of money and of lands. Eight million acres of national land

have been given to scientific schools in different
States. The common schools are supported
either by annual grants from the State treasury,
or by taxes levied directly upon the inhabitants
of each school-district. Hence the privileges of
the schools are either free to the pupils, or are
furnished at a very slight cost.

By general consent, the Bible was, for a long
time, read in the public schools as a daily exercise; or the schools were opened with the sing-
ing of a hymn and the repetition of the Lord's
Prayer: but, this being objected to by Roman
Catholics, the custom has been in many cases
abandoned, or modified to meet their prejudices.
The following extracts from the " Code of Public
Instruction in the State of New York " set forth
the principles upon which specific religious instruction is excluded from the public schools: —

" The object of the common-school system of
this State is to afford means of secular instruction to all children over five and under twenty-
one years of age resident therein. For their
religious training the State does not provide,
and with this it does not interfere. The advantages of the school are to be free to all alike.

No distinction is to be made between Christians, whether Protestants or Romanists; and the consciences of none can be legally violated. There is no authority in the law to use, as a matter of right, any portion of the regular school-hours in conducting any religious exercises at which the attendance of the scholars is made compulsory. On the other hand, there is nothing to prevent the reading of the Scriptures, or the performance of other religious exercises by the teacher, in the presence of such of the scholars as may attend voluntarily, or by the direction of their parents or guardians, if this be done before the hour fixed for the opening of the school, or after the dismissal of the school.

" Neither the common-school system nor any other social system can be maintained unless the conscientious views of all are equally respected. The simple rule, so to exercise your own right as not to infringe on those of others, will preserve equal justice among all, promote harmony, and insure success to our schools.

" The money to support schools comes from the people at large, irrespective of sect or denomination. Consequently, instruction of a sectarian or religious-denominational character must be avoided; and teachers must conform themselves, during school-hours, to their legitimate and proper duties."

These principles are now generally accepted and practically observed. But it is fairly within the province of the teacher to give instruction in the historical portions of the Bible, in the history of Christianity and of other religions, and also in the principles of ethics and the rules of moral action as these have been developed under Christian civilization. The attempt of the Roman Catholics to pervert the schools to their own ends will not be endured by the American people. The moral tone of the school will depend very much upon the character and spirit of the teacher, and his wisdom in imparting counsel without recourse to dogma.*

It would be a great mistake to infer, that, for

---

* For a full statement of the relations of the common schools in the United States to religion and morality, the author refers to his testimony given to the Educational Commission of the British Parliament for Manchester and Salisbury, and published in the Parliamentary Blue Book for 1853.

lack of a positive confessional training in the public schools, children in the United States grow up in ignorance of the truths of religion : on the contrary, in no country are the children better instructed in religion than are the children of the *native* population in the United States. Though legal decisions have been rendered against any formal religious instruction in schools supported by the State, yet the lack of such instruction in the common schools is largely supplied by means of Sunday schools, which are supported voluntarily by the churches, and into which at least five millions of children are freely gathered to be taught religious truth. These schools are the nurseries of piety for the Church, and of morality for the State.

## SECTION VII.

### SUMMARY OF PRINCIPLES AND RESULTS.

§ 1. *General Principles.* — Our analysis and discussion have brought out the following principles as fundamental to the relations of Church and State in the United States : —

(1.) Religious liberty is everywhere recognized as an absolute personal right. Religious toleration is simply a concession by the State to Dissenters ; but, by the American doctrine, the State has no authority over conscience, and therefore can make no concessions within the proper domain of conscience. " Toleration is not the opposite of intolerance, but is the counterfeit of it. Both are despotisms. The one assumes to itself the right of withholding liberty of conscience ; the other, of granting it." The American theory admits of neither. In the Virginia Declaration of Rights, James Madison proposed for the phrase, " All men should enjoy the fullest *toleration* in the exercise of religion," the words, " All men *are equally entitled* to the free exercise of religion ; " and thus he formulated the principle of religious liberty in all its length and breadth. Freedom of thought and speech on religion, freedom of religious faith and worship, freedom of religious association, — these are rights which the State cannot give, and must not restrict. The rights are derived from God, and from the spiritual nature of man : they inhere in the subject-matter of religion, which demands unrestricted intercourse between the soul and God. The State should recognize these rights, and protect them, but cannot interfere with them.

(2.) As a corollary from this fundamental principle, the American doctrine teaches that no religious test shall be attached to any of the functions or privileges of the citizen.

(3.) No form of belief or worship shall be set up, endowed, or patronized, by the State ; not only no one form, but no two nor ten forms, — no form whatever.

(4.) No man shall be restrained in his own

belief or disbelief by any civil penalty or proscription.

(5.) No man shall be taxed directly or indi-
rectly, or in any way compelled, for the support
of the religion of another.

§ 2. *Anomalies in Practice.* — The practice of
the American people has not always been up to
this high theoretical standard. But, on the
other hand, the doctrine of religious liberty was
not an original thesis of political philosophy
laid down by the founders of American society,
but grew out of divers methods and experiences
which were more than a century in evolving
this final formula. Hence the earlier relations
of Church and State in the Colonies present
anomalies in legislation, which became so fixed
in the habits of the people, that laws and
usages now seen to be incongruous with a perfect theory of free government were retained
in some of the States for a considerable period
after the war of Independence. Such incon-
gruities are more and more pruned away, leaving the principle of religious liberty to its
normal and healthy growth.

§ 3. *Qualifications of the Principle.* — As in

physics, so in ethics, the abstract principles of philosophy sometimes call for qualifications or compensations in practice. Religious liberty must not be abused to immoral practices nor to treasonable ends. For self-preservation, for social order, for public decency, the State must suppress vice or treason, and punish the offenders, however loudly they may profess to obey their consciences. The American people know how to respect scruples of conscience when these take the form of " passive obedience " to an obnoxious law; as, for instance, in the Quaker, who refuses to pay taxes, or to perform military service, but makes no resistance to the officer who levies upon his goods, or restrains him of his liberty. But the defiant resistance of the Mormons to United-States laws and courts will be put down by force, without respect to the plea of religion. The American people honor the sentiment of Peter, that " it is right to obey God rather than man ; " and they applaud the heroic protest of Luther at Worms, " *Hier stehe ich : ich kann nicht anders; Gott helfe mir.*" But when the god set higher than man is a foreign potentate, who asserts his supremacy over the State ; when the conscience that claims to be inviolate is a church embodied as a political infallibility, and enthroned above all civil laws and institutions, — then the people say, " Society has rights as sacred as the rights of conscience. Government, no less than religion, is from God. Conscience shall not harbor conspiracy ; religion shall not foster revolution ; your pious devotion shall not plot our destruction." One may preach polygamy as the ideal paradise of Mohammed, and may predict the millennium of the seraglio ; but he may not put his theory into practice under pain of the penitentiary. One may preach a theocracy as the ideal form of government, and, like the Millenarian fanatics of the seventeenth century — the " Fifth - Monarchy Men " — in England, or the Anabaptists of Münster in the sixteenth, may prophesy that the " stone cut without hands " is soon to dash to pieces all the governments of the world ; but woe betide him who should attempt to dash that stone against the Constitution of the United States ! The State concedes to every citizen the right to carry his religious notions to the extreme of folly, his religious practice to the extravagance of enthusiasm. So long as his actions are harmless, his vagaries are left to the corrective of public discussion. He may pretend to have received from heaven the torch of truth, and may wave this aloft to enlighten the world; but if he should fire the library, the treasury, the capitol, he would find that liberty itself has an asylum for the madman, a prison for the incendiary, a gallows for the traitor.

§ 4. *Traits of American Character.* — Americans are sometimes thought to be indifferent to any thing beyond their present material interests, and also to have a weakness for novelties and extravagances which makes them the dupes of spiritual imposture. Hence many in Europe believe either that the United States will be given over to the delusions of Spiritualism, Mormonism, &c., or will yet fall a prey to the machinations of the Jesuits, through the very liberty which the people are too indifferent to conserve. That promiscuous book-maker, Hepworth Dixon, has been taken for an authority; and his jackal propensity for social carrion — shown also in his book on Russia — has been transferred to the nation which he has slandered.

As to Mormonism, so far as the native population of the United States are concerned, this has had its day. Though this fungus has fastened itself upon the tree of American liberty, it draws its sustenance from foreign roots. The whole population of Utah is less than ninety thousand : of these, thirty thousand are of foreign birth ; and of the remainder, full sixty per cent are children of foreign parents. The ratio of residents not Mormons is now rapidly increasing since the completion of the Pacific Railroad ; and the popular conviction in the United States is, that the Mormon community, hemmed in by a normal society, will die of inanition. Many dupes of the system are ready to abandon it ; and the death of Brigham Young might lead to the disintegration of the community. President Grant is disposed to try what resources there may be in United-States law for bringing the Mormons under the common social order of the republic ; but public sentiment would leave the delusion to a natural death. In any event, it is doomed.

As to Spiritualism, this, under all its phases, allures but a small percentage of the American people. The system is not more prevalent in the United States than in some countries of Europe ; though the American habit of public discussion has made it more prominent.

The growth of Romanism in the United States may give more serious cause for anxiety ; * but this also has been exaggerated through fear, and by overlooking some compensating elements of the problem. True, the fact stares us in the face, that the Roman Catholics have trebled their churches in the last twenty years.

|  | Churches. | Value. |
|---|---|---|
| In 1850, | 1,222 | $9,256,758 |
| " 1860, | 2,550 | 26,774,119 |
| " 1870, | 3,806 | 60,985,566 |

The great increase of value is due to the enhancement of all property since the war, and to the fact that the Roman-Catholic churches are chiefly in the cities. Hence, though their church-property represents a sixth of the total valuation of church-property in the country, in

* For a good discussion of this subject, the reader is referred to the valuable articles of Dr. Friedrich Kapp in the *Gegenwart* for March, 1873.

point of number their churches are only a sixteenth of the whole. The Roman Catholics claim five million adherents; but, by the natural ratio of births, they should have at least a million more. Many drop away from their communion, whose loss is never reported; while the few proselytes from Protestantism are trumpeted abroad.

Moreover, the Irish immigration, which has been the main feeder of the Roman-Catholic Church in the United States, has reached its maximum, and shows symptoms of decline. The German immigration, fifty per cent of which is Protestant, already exceeds it; and the improved condition of Ireland will tend to keep her population at home.*

With the growing consciousness of numbers and of wealth, the Roman-Catholic Church in the United States becomes more arrogant in its utterances. One incidental effect of the separation of the Roman-Catholic Church from the State is to make its clergy more absolutely dependent upon Rome. With

---

* For the German element in the United States, see Appendix II.

no temporal prince to fall back upon, they bow implicitly to the mandates of the pope. Hence American prelates voted for the infallibility dogma; and the most intellectual organ of that church in New York asserts the authority of the Church over the State, even in civil concerns. "While the State has rights, she has them only in virtue and by permission of the superior authority: and that authority can only be expressed through the Church; that is, through the organic law infallibly announced and unchangeably asserted, regardless of temporal consequences." * The power of the ballot, wielded by Catholic hands, is invoked to establish this authority of the Church. Now, the American people are long-suffering. It is too much their habit to trust in the *laisser-faire* policy. Like Mr. Micawber, they wait for "something to turn up," and leave things to take their course. Hence the plotters of mischief may, for a time, have their own way.

Moreover, the American citizen is apt to be too intent upon his own affairs to give much

* The Catholic World, July, 1872.

heed to affairs of State. He is pre-occupied with his own calling. The apostolic precept which he most devoutly fulfils is "to provide for his own." Hence "rings" can work their way into office, and Jesuits can hatch conspiracies, because the better class of citizens are too busy to take note of them.

These two characteristics of the American people often cause them to be misunderstood at home and abroad. But deeper than these, and stronger by far, is a sterling devotion to right, justice, law, government; and when these are invaded or threatened, when society is in peril, when government is assailed, when the foundations of public order are disturbed, then these same men who have been so eager in their own affairs, so easy-going toward public affairs, will drop all private business, and take things into their own hands with a tremendous energy of purpose, and tenacity of will, that nothing can withstand. Thus slavery was demolished; thus the New-York ring was broken and scattered; and thus, too, will political Romanism be trampled out.

The loyalty of Americans is hard to be un-

derstood in Europe, because it presents nothing
that is tangible ; but, in this very loyalty to an
ideal, the practical Americans show the philo-
sophic side of their character.   The Pilgrim
Fathers brought with them the Church and the
State, each as a spiritual essence, but also as a
living power.   Three thousand miles behind
them they had left bishops and clergy, cathe-
dral and ritual, the pomp and circumstance of
the Establishment ; but there, in the cabin of
" The Mayflower," was the church of believing, praying souls, borne, as of old, in the ark
above the flood, and with the holy dove as its
symbol of peace.   Three thousand miles behind
them they had left king and nobles, parliament
and courts, all the insignia of government ; but
there, in the cabin of " The Mayflower," was
the primordial State, the sentiment of justice,
of order, of law, enthroning itself in an authority chosen by the whole for the good of the
whole.   The dialectic mind of the American
people is much given to such abstractions of
ethical and political philosophy ; and nowhere
have these been more refined upon, or more
sharply defined.   Yet these abstractions stand

forth as concrete realities, when law, government, liberty, are assailed; and then the practical American will fight for them against all comers. This the Romish hierarchy may one day learn to their cost, if they shall presume too far upon the indifference of the public to affairs of state. Germany and Italy, battling for state independence of ecclesiastical control, need have no fear that the doctrine of Papal supremacy will be suffered to intrench itself behind Church independence in the United States.

§ 5. *American Nationality against Church Prerogative.* — This assurance is based upon the inherent nationality of the American people as this has developed under more than two centuries and a half. There are publicists in Europe who persist in regarding the political life of the American people as an experiment; and there are ethnologists who look upon their national life as an embryo, which, in its nascent or plastic state, is yet to be shaped by the influence of foreign immigration; the very being of American society to be moulded by influences from England, Ireland, and Germany. But nothing could be more contrary to the facts of history and science than such surmises.

The organic life of the American nation, indeed, is but little more than two and a half centuries ; but the founders of American society carried with them all the fruits of civilization from what was then the foremost race of Christendom. Moreover, the confederation of the New-England Colonies, by which they declared, that " as in nation and religion, so in other respects, we be and continue one," — this league of Englishmen in America for civil liberty and the Protestant faith was older than the peace of Westphalia, by which the Holy Roman Empire received its death-blow, and the foundation was laid for a new Germany. The uprising of New England for Protestant liberty in 1689 preceded by twelve years the erection of Prussia into a kingdom ; and the final uprising of all the Colonies for liberty and independence was contemporary with the peaceful consolidation of Prussia in the closing years of Frederic the Great.

If nationality is determined by an original race-stock sufficiently positive and vigorous to assimilate all foreign elements with its own individuality, then America has a nationality. If this is determined by one language speaking through the laws, through the press, through the schools, through the pulpit, and compelling the homage of all native dialects and all foreign tongues, then America has a nationality through the noble speech of Shakspeare, of Milton, and of Burke, — a language rich in the traditions of liberty, and whose literature breathes more of the spirit of humanity, of freedom, and of Christianity, than any other of the tongues of men. If a literature is a mark of nationality, America has this in poets, preachers, philosophers, novelists, historians, of indigenous growth, whose names are household words at home, and whose works are sought for libraries abroad. If a history gives the stamp of nationality, then the history of the American people, marking the progress of the same ideas, and illustrious with successful wars of principle, is not an outline of political and social theories, but the history of a nation, with its talismanic legends and heroes. "Lexington is none the worse to me for not being in

Greece, nor Gettysburg that its name is not Marathon."

American nationality was not created by a constitution : it is the growth of institutions, or rather of principles and ideas rooted in the hearts of the people. The Constitution was the natural expression of that homogeneous national life which had then been maturing for more than a century, and which prompted the sublime declaration of the preamble : " We the people of the United States, in order to form a more perfect union, establish justice, insure domestic tranquillity, promote the general welfare, and secure the blessings of liberty to ourselves and our posterity, do ordain and establish this Constitution for the United States of America." Back of the Constitution there is a people, back of the Union a national life ; and priestcraft would seek in vain to deceive the one, or to destroy the other. The pope can no more Romanize America than he could revolutionize Germany.

## CONCLUSION.

To sum up all in one word, in the United States *religion depends upon the moral power of light and love, and not upon the arm of the law.* And in this, as in other interests of society, freedom develops the responsibility which is vigilance, the activity which is life, and the union which is strength. Such is the solution of the problem of Church and State in America. But as God has not given to any man to possess all genius and grace in his own mind and person, neither has he given to any nation to possess all perfection in race, religion, society, and government. Travel in many lands, and acquaintance with various peoples, have taught me that beneath all forms and institutions flows the life-current of humanity ; and that in every hand, if only one learns to clasp it rightly, beats the pulse of brotherhood. But nowhere have I

so felt the thrill of this common life as upon
the soil of Germany in 1866, and now again in
1873. The conflicts of Germany for her national
unity and her spiritual independence stir the
heart of an American like watchwords from his
own Heimath. And is not the voice, the spirit,
the life, common to both countries? Says Freeman, " The institutions which were once common to the whole Teutonic race contain the
germs out of which every free constitution in
the world has grown." * Those ancient free
institutions have held their own in England;
and America has inherited them divested of later appendages. And German and American,
pointing proudly back to the free spirit of a
common ancestry, can say, " Our ancient history
is the possession of the liberal, who, as being
ever ready to reform, is the true conservative;
not of the self-styled conservative, who, by
refusing to reform, does all he can to bring on
destruction." It is the revival of the old Teutonic spirit of conservative progress that has
made Germany the astonishment of Europe

* Freeman: Growth of the English Constitution.

and the admiration of America. May God grant to her to solve peaceably the gravest problem of modern society! — How shall the State give liberty without losing it in the very act of giving it?

APPENDIX.

# APPENDIX.

---

## APPENDIX I. — PAGE 119.

### THE AMERICAN THANKSGIVING.

THANKSGIVING, as a yearly festival for the ingathering of the harvest, was instituted by the Pilgrims soon after the settlement of Plymouth. It was imitated by the other Colonies of New England, and for a long time was known as the New-England festival. By degrees, its obvious propriety, and its happy associations as a family feast, caused it to be adopted in other parts of the country. At length, during the late war, President Lincoln exalted it to a national festival; and as such it is now welcomed over all the land. Special days of thanksgiving were also observed upon memorable occasions; and it is an interesting fact, that, in 1632, the government of Massachusetts twice appointed a public thanksgiving for the successes of the Protestants in Germany under Gustavus Adolphus.

The yearly Thanksgiving is no sectional festival. So abundant are the fruits of the land, so diversified the products of the several States, that each and all have cause for thanksgiving without jealousy of others. It is no sectarian observance. Whatever God is acknowledged and worshipped, — the God of Christian or of Jew, of the philosophical Deist, or of the believer in a supernatural revelation, — every man's God, even "Nature" herself, may be thanked and praised in such a festival, as the source of all good. It is a household festival, which gathers around it the fond ties of family union, the blessed memories of the sainted dead, the tokens of parental and of filial love. The gray hairs of age, the roses of youth, the buds of infancy, are woven together in its crown, — the evergreen remembrances of the past, the fresh-blooming hopes of the future. The Anglo-Saxon race is rooted in the home.

This is a feast of brotherhood. Good-feeling abounds, and shows itself in caring for the needy, the widow, the orphan. Every hospital, every poor-house, every mission-station, shares in the festival: even the prisoner is cheered on this day with some relaxation of his confinement, some remembrance from the outside world.

It is a festival of devotion, which recalls men from their own labors, and from all the wondrous operations of Nature, back to the God and Father of all, from whom cometh every good and every perfect gift. Unsectional, unsectarian, uniting the three chief elements of society, — home, humanity, religion, — this festival may well stand before the world as a picture of American character and life.

## APPENDIX II. — Page 143.

### THE GERMAN POPULATION IN THE UNITED STATES.

[In the summer of 1872, the author read before the Geograph-
ical Society of Berlin a paper on the Physical Geography of the
United States as a Moment for National Unity. Some allusions
in that paper to the number and the influence of the German
population led to a discussion, in consequence of which the author prepared for the society a second paper, the substance of
which is given in this Appendix.]

It is a common notion that the increase of population in the United States is chiefly from European
immigration. For instance, in the popular Geography of Daniel one reads, "The number of inhabitants in the United States, which is steadily
increased by emigration from Europe, reaches nearly
forty million. Of these, five million are colored, and
over thirty million white, of which about one-third
are German." One-third; that is, ten millions Germans! So far Daniel's Geography. But what is the
fact? The census for 1870 returns only 1,690,533

native Germans. To these should be added, for the children of German parents and of German and American parents now living in the United States, 3,300,000; giving for the total German element, pure and mixed, about 5,000,000.

The census gives a grand total of 10,892,015 persons now living in the United States, whose parents, one or both, were of foreign birth. But about one-half of these are children of English-speaking parents, and the remainder grow up with the English language and with American ideas; and *their* children will lose almost all trace of a foreign ancestry. Hence neither the language nor the race-stock of the American people is likely to be seriously impaired by immigration.

By the census of 1870, the whole number of persons of foreign birth in the United States is 5,566,-546. These are classified by nationalities as follows: England, 550,924; Scotland, 140,835; Wales, 74,533; Ireland, 1,855,827; Germany, 1,690,533; France, 116,402; Spain, 3,764; Italy, 17,157; Sweden and Norway, 211,578; other countries of Europe, 180,646; British America, 492,195; China, 63,100; all others, 308,938. But the previous census of 1860 showed, that, in the forty years preceding (that is, from 1820 to 1860), the number of immigrants to the United States was 5,062,414: of

11

these Great Britain furnished 2,750,874, and Germany 1,546,476. In the ten years from 1860 to 1870, the period of the war, the total immigration was less by 342,105 than in the decade from 1850 to 1860. The ratio of German immigration has gained somewhat upon the Irish; but, during the last decade, the rate of mortality among male adults was much increased by the war, in which the Germans bore an honorable part. The number of persons living in the United States in 1870, who were born in foreign countries, is barely half a million more than the whole number of immigrants from 1820 to 1860. In the fifty years from 1820 to 1870, about two millions of the registered immigrants have disappeared by death or return.

Mr. Louis Schade has put forth the theory that the native stock of the United States is declining in productiveness, and that the rate of increase among the foreign population is fast gaining upon it. Dr. Frederic Kapp, whose opinion is entitled to great respect, has adopted the same theory. But Mr. Edward Jarvis, in "The Atlantic Monthly" for April, 1872, from a mathematical analysis of the best tables, has demonstrated that this theory of Schade was based upon inaccurate data; that the natural increase is at a lower rate in the foreign than in the American families; and that, in the whole white population, the purely American element exceeds seventy per cent. This is, perhaps, an over-estimate.

The first official census of the United States was in 1790; and a careful comparison of the census of 1870 gives the following result : —

Native-born descendants from the population of 1790, 62 per cent.
    (Of these forty-nine per cent are whites, and thir-
       teen per cent colored.)
Native-born from foreign parents . . . . . 24   "
                         —
Total of native born . . . . . . . . 86   "
Foreign born . . . . . . . . . 14   "

This gives in the whole population five of native stock to three of foreign and the children of foreign, nine of the same stock to two of foreign birth, and six born upon the soil of the United States, of every parentage, to one born in foreign lands. Moreover, all the influences of climate, of society, of education, of language, of intermarriage, combine to *Americanize* the children of immigrants; and the qualities of the dominant race prevail, in the end, above all mixtures and crossings. A foreign people, — as, for instance, the Cubans or the Mexicans, — if annexed bodily to the United States, might perpetuate their race, their language, and their customs, to the prejudice of American ideas and institutions, and, per-

haps, to the peril of American unity.  Such annexation is of doubtful policy.  In immigration, however,
the process is not one of annexation, but of absorp-
tion; and, thus far, " Uncle Sam " is proved to have a
digestion strong enough for a very mixed diet.  Immigrants are not taken up by nations nor by ship-
loads, but each particular immigrant is absorbed as a
separate molecule, and thus the vast total of the
foreign element is fused into the body politic in harmony with the life of the national organism.

If one takes into account the facility with which
this cosmopolitan nation appropriates foreign elements, and the vital force by which it assimilates
them all, it will appear that the Americans have
hardly less of race unity than the English, — the
outcome of so many immigrations and invasions, con-
fusing diverse foreign peoples with the primitive
island stock, till at last, after the Norman conquest,
all elements were fused into the English nation.
For the United States are neither, like Austria, an
agglomeration, nor, like Turkey, a conglomeration, of
different nationalities, nor, like the Roman empire,
a union of races effected through the pressure of
conquest and annexation; but the individual forms
of these numerous and various foreign elements are
fused with the mass of the original metal; and,
though the process may leave much slag, the mass

retains enough of its original character readily to identify its nature and source.

As the English Colonies in North America by degrees supplanted the Spanish, French, and Dutch settlements, and either exterminated or absorbed them, there came to be in the whole land a preponderating English stock, which, through its spirit, its ideas, its institutions, and indeed through the quality of its blood, impressed its features and character upon the young and growing nation; and hence the American race of to-day, however modified through foreign mixture and by the nerve-properties of climate, is only a sprout of the Anglo-Saxon stock, which, all fresh and vigorous, asserts its Darwinian right to exist. The argument for national identity derived from race has certainly as much weight for the people of the United States as for the people of Spain.

The Visigoths, to the number of many hundred thousands, overran Spain, and, for more than two centuries, held the country as conquerors; and, though they were conquered in turn, they were never expelled. Yet, while their influence may be traced in that corruption of the Latin which preceded the formation of the Spanish tongue, and their blood mingles in the veins of multitudes of Spaniards, the German character was not stamped upon the Spanish race. The conquering race was fused into the conquered. Much less will the modern invasion of America by Germany efface the characteristics of the American people. Acting like a transfusion by vivisection, it may bring out in a more pronounced type the primitive atavism of both varieties; but in a few generations the descendants of the German-Americans of to-day will obey the laws of race, of history, and of destiny, and become, in language, in manners, in ideas, and also in physique and physiognomy, *Americans.*

Americans would be sorry to estimate the average intelligence and culture of the German people by the bulk of German immigrants. Many of these are slow to comprehend two characteristics which are deeply fixed in the American stock, and which have given strength and stability to American institutions, — reverence for the authority of law, and respect for the teachings and the usages of religion. In the main, however, the German element mixes well with the American; and it is highly valued on account of the industry and thrift of the lower classes, and of the cultivation in science, literature, and art, so often found in the higher.